# HOW TO START
# A BUSINESS
## ON YOUR
### Kitchen Table

# HOW TO START
# A BUSINESS
## ON YOUR
## Kitchen Table

### SHANN NIX JONES

**HAY HOUSE**

Carlsbad, California • New York City
London • Sydney • New Delhi

**Published in the United Kingdom by:**
Hay House UK Ltd, The Sixth Floor, Watson House,
54 Baker Street, London W1U 7BU
Tel: +44 (0)20 3927 7290; Fax: +44 (0)20 3927 7291
www.hayhouse.co.uk

**Published in the United States of America by:**
Hay House Inc., PO Box 5100, Carlsbad, CA 92018-5100
Tel: (1) 760 431 7695 or (800) 654 5126
Fax: (1) 760 431 6948 or (800) 650 5115; www.hayhouse.com

**Published in Australia by:**
Hay House Australia Pty Ltd, 18/36 Ralph St, Alexandria NSW 2015
Tel: (61) 2 9669 4299; Fax: (61) 2 9669 4144; www.hayhouse.com.au

**Published in India by:**
Hay House Publishers India, Muskaan Complex,
Plot No.3, B-2, Vasant Kunj, New Delhi 110 070
Tel: (91) 11 4176 1620; Fax: (91) 11 4176 1630; www.hayhouse.co.in

A catalogue record for this book is available from the British Library.

Tradepaper ISBN: 978-1-78817-378-0
E-book ISBN: 978-1-78817-409-1
Audiobook ISBN: 978-1-78817-439-8

Printed and bound by
CPI Group (UK) Ltd, Croydon, CR0 4YY

# CONTENTS

*'Ask what makes you come alive, and go do it.
Because what the world needs is
people who have come alive.'*

Howard W. Thurman, philosopher and civil rights leader

*'We rise by lifting others.'*

Robert Ingersoll, writer

*'Juicily pro-living a life FULL of adventures.
YES MAAATE!!!'*

Belinda Knott, WATT sister

# PROLOGUE

As we were waiting for this book to be published, coronavirus happened.

In the space of 12 weeks, life as we knew it came screeching to a halt. As I write this, countries that represent over 50 per cent of the world's global GDP are closed for business. Experts say that our economy is currently teetering on the brink of collapse, heading towards the deepest recession in living memory.

I first conceived this book in the wake of the 'Amazon asteroid', which changed the entire business environment. Now coronavirus has changed the entire landscape again. When the world fully emerges from lockdown, the environment will look completely different. It's hard to say what the new requirements for success will be.

So, what's the only thing that can save you, when the environment is constantly shifting under your feet?

Resilience.

Imagine the dinosaurs' landscape after the original asteroid hit. Everything breaking, cracking, shifting... lava crevasses opening abruptly, a completely altered environment that continued to change as you watched. Any organism that was unable to adapt, perished.

It's the same today. If you've lost your job, the parameters of your life have changed or you simply feel called to do something new in the post-coronavirus world, this book is for you. It provides a value-based toolkit to help you create a new way of being in the new reality, whatever that may be.

It's time to start again, and this time to do it your way.

The only safe orientation is an internal one. You must readjust to your internal compass. Align yourself to your heart, and align your heart to the heart of the world. This will make sure that you have integrity with what's required, even as those requirements change.

Don't be afraid to reinvent yourself. Reinvention in the face of change is the way forward. We're being called into something new, something creative, something that the world has never seen before.

This is a mantra I relied on, during the period of crazy shifts, to keep me aligned and agile, responsive to change:

I connect.

I engage.

I surrender.

I respond.

Coronavirus, and the economic chaos that ensued after global lockdown, was horrible, unspeakable. No one would have wished for it. But it also did something amazing – it wiped the slate clean. It forced us to begin again, because everything that existed before was gone.

So, what are you going to do about it? How will you connect, engage, surrender, respond?

This challenge is an incalculable gift.

The world is calling you forward, as never before. If you were afraid – afraid of quitting your job, afraid of taking a risk, afraid of upsetting the status quo – don't be. Because there is no status quo. Not any more.

This is your time. Because now you have a guidance tool that's guaranteed to work in this new and unfamiliar landscape – it's the Five Directions compass I introduce in Step 4 (*see page 54*). The intersection of what you love, what you're good at, what the world needs, what you can make money doing and what the Universe is pushing you towards – this is where you need to head. This internal magnetic North is unaffected by disease, disaster or economic crisis.

The advice here works. It's stress-tested. It worked to take our business through coronavirus in a halo of safety. During lockdown we continued to trade, by special permission of the Welsh Assembly Government. In fact, our business increased by 50 per cent. Despite our small size, we were even able to donate more than £100,000 worth of our healing products to brave NHS frontline doctors and nurses. To achieve this, we had to increase our skincare production by 200 per cent, but we managed it. Someone called us 'The Little Company That Gives'. I couldn't be more proud of any title.

So, what worked? For us, it was all about using value-based principles for guidance. Chuckling Goat is the exact intersection of what we love, what we're good at, what the world needs, and products and services for which we can be paid. It's also aligned with the direction in which the Universe was pushing us.

Because we use the Five Direction compass, we kept asking the question: 'What does the world need right now?' and we kept pivoting towards the answer. This is the basis of our business model – not cash flow or return on investment. As a result, we continued to function at a high performance level during the crisis. We're living proof that you can do well by doing good. Here's how we did it:

- **Offer real value.** Our business improves people's health. When lockdown hit, the Welsh Assembly Government gave us permission to continue trading, because our products were helpful.

- **Expect change.** Everything changes. This is the one thing I know for sure – whatever is happening now is about to change. Be prepared to shift, move, adjust. The advantage of a small business is that it can be lighter than air, and agile when it comes to change.

- **Ask, 'How is this an opportunity?'** Because the NHS was busy taking care of those who were critically ill, lots of other people started improving their own gut health in order to proactively boost their immune system. We were there to help.

- **Always communicate.** Because we don't sell through outside retailers, we were able to stay in intimate contact with our own customers. I started writing two content-based newsletters every week to stay in touch – people loved it, and it strengthened our relationships.

- **Never compromise.** We built our business on the core values of caring for our animals, our family, our team, our environment and our customers. This created a value crystal that was solid, and not distorted. When we grew that crystal into a palisade big enough to protect our family and our team, it held, because it had integrity.

We're entering a new world. It's time for you to get out there and help make it a better place.

Luckily for you, you already have everything you need to succeed! So take my hand, and let's go there – together.

*Shann Nix Jones*

12 June 2020

# INTRODUCTION

Welcome, my sweet friend. You're amazing. And finally, it's your time. Welcome to the Age of the Butterfly.

How did we get here? First, the 'Amazon asteroid' killed the high street. In 2006, Amazon launched Fulfilment by Amazon, which gave small businesses the ability to use Amazon's own order fulfilment and customer service infrastructure. Bricks-and-mortar retail giants shuddered, and the high street began to die. In 2008, the fall of Woolworths, which had been a major presence on UK high streets for almost 100 years, sent shock waves across the nation. Over the next decade, 32 major UK retailers closed their doors for good.

Then, in January 2020, coronavirus hit, followed rapidly by global lockdown. This simply wrapped up the job that Amazon started. Coronavirus underscored the 'online is the right line' trend that was already in place. Businesses that were already trading online found it easier to keep going. Businesses that weren't online and weren't considered essential, shut down. Some closed their doors temporarily; some closed forever.

Turns out, the Internet has impacted the business world in the same way that the asteroid once impacted the dinosaurs. That's to say, it changed everything.

And it's created the same result as the original asteroid that wiped out the dinosaurs 66 million years ago: smaller animals have taken over the landscape once dominated by the lumbering Stegosaurus and the hulking T-Rex. I call them 'butterfly businesses': small, quick, colourful, lighter than air – many of them run by women.

## An exciting new landscape

Consider the following statistics, released by US-based small-business support network SCORE in 2018. They paint a slightly different picture than the doom-and-gloom figures coming from the rest of the business world in the same year. They reveal that:

- Women are slightly more likely than men to start businesses.

- 57 per cent of women business owners expected their revenues to increase in 2018.

- 27 per cent of women-owned businesses hired employees in 2018.

- 29 per cent of female entrepreneurs said their business was expanding moderately.

- Just 2 per cent of women expect revenues to decrease by more than 20 per cent.

- 62 per cent of women entrepreneurs said their business was their primary income source, challenging old assumptions that women entrepreneurs are more likely to run lifestyle businesses that provide supplemental income.

- Women are more likely than men to launch businesses in healthcare and education.

- Just 25 per cent of women sought financing for their business. This is a significantly lower proportion than the 34 per cent of men who sought funding for their business.

- 5 per cent of female entrepreneurs said their business was expanding aggressively.

I'm one of those women. Back in 2014, I started making soap, lotion and goat's milk kefir on our kitchen table. Four years later, our little family business had a turnover of more than £4 million. Now we have 22 employees and ship our product to hundreds of thousands of customers in 51 countries across the globe. How did we do it?

By ignoring every piece of traditional business advice we ever received. And by using instead a set of value-based ideas that I'm going to share with you in this book.

## Avoiding 'the suits'

Personally, I always loathed the idea of conventional 'business', because I never liked the values that seemed to go along with it. It appeared to me to be a lot of white guys wearing grey suits and red ties, babbling on about Q1 and Q2, crushing the competition and stabbing one another in the back. Dinosaur-eat-dinosaur. And we all know what happened to the dinosaurs! It wasn't that appealing, and not a world I ever wanted to inhabit.

Plus, I never understood anything about business plans, so I thought I couldn't run a business. Here's a funny secret, don't tell anyone – four years and a £1 million annual profit later, I still don't understand business plans! I still couldn't write one, even if you put my head in a bag and threatened to take away my afternoon cup of tea! The closest I ever got was reading *Business Plans for Dummies* on the train on the way to meet with an investor. I didn't finish it. Turns out that unless you're trying to get a loan, you don't really need to know about business plans!

So, what's so great about running your own business, and why am I trying to convince you to go ahead and take this risk? Because I can honestly put my hand on my heart and say that no matter what actually happens with your business, you'll never regret having jumped off that cliff. Running your own business, whether it ultimately succeeds or fails, is an astonishing journey that will enrich your life, and teach you things you never knew you needed to learn. Running your own business does everything that personal therapy does, but faster.

### Running your own business will teach you important lessons about yourself.

Do you have fears about your own abilities, negative beliefs that are holding you back, old wounds, griefs, doubts, fears of failure?

Run your own business! The process will put those issues right up in your face – and demand that you solve them. Quickly. No need to spend 10 years on the therapy coach – everything you need to fix is going to bubble to the surface, and will insist on being addressed. You'll sort yourself out and start moving forward along your own life path, faster than you ever believed possible.

And here's the wonderful secret – *you don't need to know everything when you start.*

It's exactly like having a baby or caring for a pet – you don't know everything, when you start. You couldn't possibly, even if you have an MBA (which I don't!).

The trick is that you'll learn what you need to know, as you go. The journey itself will be your teacher. The process is the practice. All you need is the courage to put your boots on the road and take that very first step.

I love coaching women who want to run their own businesses, because I love to watch the process of smart people aligning themselves to live their own best lives. The way I see it, success is about living according to your values. Not my values – not anyone else's values. But your very own values. Whatever they may be.

Your *life* is your business. You're the CEO of your own destiny.

## A working life that's based on your values

If you can create a life in which you live and work in such a way that you address your very own values, every day – then you're a success. It has nothing to do with money. You just need to have a passion, and a drive to offer real value in the world.

So let me offer you an alternative definition of business. In my opinion, real business isn't about getting ahead of the competition, or doing sleazy marketing, or betraying your values, or even accumulating vast amounts of wealth.

The real point of business is *walking your gift out into the world*.

Don't get me wrong – there's nothing wrong with wealth. It can purchase some useful things, like peace and freedom and security for your family. But I believe we've had it backwards all this time. Business isn't for making money. Sure, the money is great. But the money isn't the point.

Business, pursued properly, can be about making a commitment to walking your gift into the world. Just as you'd advocate for your child, you need to advocate for your business.

A lot of women in my Women at the Table support group for female entrepreneurs (or 'WATT' for short) say that they're hesitant to put themselves out there, to 'big' themselves up. This creates a deep conflict in them, when it's time to market their business, to set their prices, to connect with customers.

So here's what I tell them: It's not about you. *It's about giving a gift*.

## Starting your own business is about bringing your gift to the world.

Exactly what that gift is (hint: it's the intersection of what you love, what you're good at, what you can be paid for, what the world needs, and what the universe has planned for you) we'll explore together, and I'm going to offer you a technique that will help you work it out.

Whatever you were put on this earth to do, it's your duty and your responsibility to fulfil that gift, to advocate for it, and to walk it bravely into the world – just as you would a beloved child. Would you feel too shy to walk your child into kindergarten and show them around their new school? No, of course not! You'd be concentrating on the child, getting them settled, introducing them to their new teachers and new classmates. Your shyness or feelings of self-consciousness simply don't come into it – you need to be there for your child.

In exactly that same way, you need to be there for your gift. Whatever it is, the world is waiting for you to express it, and if you don't, it will remain forever unexpressed. Business is simply a way of getting things done – it's a way of putting your gift out into the world.

Pioneer of modern dance Martha Graham said it best:

**'There is a vitality, a life force, a quickening that's translated through you into action, and because there is only one of you in all time, this expression is unique. And if you block it, it will never exist through any other medium and be lost.'**

You have a duty to play your part and put your puzzle piece out there, into the big global puzzle – because if you don't, no one else ever will! That piece will be lost forever.

It's about taking responsibility for making your contribution to the world. This is the great thing about butterflies – we understand something that the dinosaurs didn't. We don't favour the dinosaur-eat-dinosaur approach – because after all, look what happened to them! Butterflies don't feel the need to kill off all the other butterflies. No butterfly wants to be the only butterfly in the rainforest. We understand instinctively that the rainforest needs to be intact for all of us to thrive. We know that more butterflies can fertilize more flowers, which means more pollen, which means more flowers, which will feed more butterflies. If we look after one another, there will ultimately be more for everyone.

Cooperation, not competition. In the post-asteroid world, this is what it's all about. These days you must adapt to survive, and the old rules are as dead as the industries that followed them.

And here's the good news – you don't have to be perfect, or currently successful, or have a business degree, or even be good at maths, to run your own business. I didn't have any of those qualifications when I started my own business. Actually, I was flat broke, with no business experience, a family to look after and a sick husband to worry about.

In fact, I never intended to start a business. I wasn't the business type. I could never manage to balance my cheque book, and I had no flair for numbers whatsoever. I was an English major, a writer, a journalist, and content to be so.

## Decide on your priorities

I'm still not exactly sure how that changed, or when. I suppose it all came out of necessity, out of common sense, out of a desire to stop travelling and spend more time with my husband. It did *not* stem, ever, in any way, from a desire to make a lot of money or enter the business realm.

Here's what I wanted, in chronological order as the business developed:

1.  To spend more time with my husband, whom I met late in life.

2.  To make our little farm productive.

3.  To save my husband's life when he was ill.

4.  To create a rising tide that would raise not only our own boat, but the boats of our loved ones – our daughter, our son-in-law, my husband's brother.

5.  To help other people who were suffering, and who came to us desperate when they had been everywhere else and had failed to find aid.

You see? These are my drivers. Nowhere on that list was domination of a market or return on investment.

And yet – somehow – I seem to have created a business that had a 6000 per cent growth rate in just four years.

Here's my secret – running a business is a journey. You don't have to have it all together when you start. You simply take a deep breath and put your boots on the road, in deep faith that you'll be shown the way forward as you go. One step at a time, you travel that road. You learn what you need to know, as you go along. Baby steps will get you there.

If I did it, you can too.

## Starting a business means having faith and taking the journey step by step.

The world has changed. And while I'm not going to argue that the 'Amazon asteroid' was a good thing, I will say that it's opened the way for new ideas – butterfly ideas – to flourish. The dinosaurs crashing down has freed up a lot of air and sunlight for smaller critters to thrive. These days, it's the quick, fast-moving businesses – heart-centred, high-value, passion-based business – that are surging to the fore. Artisan businesses, boutique businesses, business driven by the desire to make a difference, rather than cash. Large numbers of women are starting these businesses and running them for new reasons – to create the lives they want, for themselves and their families. Cash is no longer king – it's all about offering value.

Welcome to the Age of the Butterfly. It's your time.

So what's the gift you have to give? And are you ready to walk it into the world?

Then take my hand and come along. We'll go on this journey together.

# *Step* 1

# CLEAR YOUR TABLE

Open and closed brain loops, and why they
matter. How to hack your own brain function
to get yourself moving forward.

Okay, so you're ready to start a business on your kitchen table. What do you need to do first?

Clear your table.

Why? Well, I know you better than you might think. I know that you're super-creative, and that you have a million ideas bouncing around in your head. I know that you're a mass of untapped potential, and that the problem is just knowing where to begin.

And I'm guessing that your dining table, right this minute, is *covered with stuff.* Am I right? Half-finished projects, unpaid bills, important stuff that hasn't been done, not-so-important stuff that's waiting to be sorted out and discarded. Maybe some children's projects or pet items there too. All the detritus of your busy life, combining potential and necessity.

## Make room for your future

So your very first assignment is to clear that table until it's completely, totally empty. Then you're going to wipe it down, go buy yourself a really beautiful handful of flowers and put those flowers in a vase. And you're going to make yourself a gut-healthy drink of your choice. And sit down and drink it, at your nice clear table.

Now, you may say, what the heck does this have to do with starting a business?

My sweet friend – *everything*. That table needs to be as clear as a runway – because that's where you're going to launch your business. And it's not going to happen from a dirty, cluttered table. Here's why:

> ### Your brain works on a series of loops.
> ### Open loops, and closed loops.
> ### Each time you start a project, your brain
> ### opens a loop. Complete that project,
> ### and the loop is closed.

The groovy technical name for this is the Zeigarnik effect. It was discovered by female Lithuanian psychologist Bluma Zeigarnik in 1927. Zeigarnik observed that waiters in a restaurant demonstrated amazing recall of which diner ordered what meal – until the plates were set down. At that point, the waiters' recall nearly completely disappeared.

This led Zeigarnik to develop the brain loop hypothesis. Turns out, taking the order opens a loop in the brain. The brain naturally wants to close the loop and complete the task. So the brain focuses attention on the task, creating the extra-sharp recall. But once the order has been completed, the loop is closed. The brain is satisfied – and the recall disappears.

It's incredibly important to understand that this is the way your brain functions, because you can use this knowledge to hack your own motivation in all kinds of ways. As you'll quickly begin to notice, open brain loops are everywhere. The heartbreak of failing to get closure when a relationship goes wrong? Open loop that hasn't been closed. A cliff-hanger on TV? Open loop. Those annoying click-through online stories? They use open loops to drive your behaviour. They ask a question that's just interesting enough to open a loop in your brain – and you'll click the button, just to close the loop.

Ernest Hemingway used this principle to drive his own writing process. When he finished writing for the day, he'd never stop at the end of a chapter – he'd always write the first line of the next chapter, thus creating an open loop to which his brain would be eager to return.

## How to 'hack in to' your own motivation

So, if you want to motivate yourself to do something, just make a start. Put on your gym clothes, for example, and your brain will want to close that loop by actually going to the gym. Need to write copy for your website? Just get down the first sentence – even if it's poorly written – and then walk away. Your brain will keep circling around that unfinished paragraph, until you're driven back to complete it the next day.

But it can work the other way, too, and have a demotivating effect. If we leave too many loops opened, we become overwhelmed by the number of open loops bobbing around in our brain. And each open loop drains energy from us. If you wake up in a messy room, each piece of clutter is essentially an open loop.

Each object left out is a decision not made, an action not completed, be it a drawer not closed or a shirt not put away: too many open loops. Every time you look at a table full of half-completed projects, un-filed letters, unpaid bills, etc, that's just a whole shed-load of open loops. The experience can be defeating. You'll lose a large percentage of your psychic energy before your feet even hit the floor. And you'll spend the day going in circles, exhausted and frazzled.

People generally tend by nature to be either loop openers or loop closers. Me, I'm an open-loop junkie. I absolutely adore the buzz of having 100 ideas, 20 books and 30 projects going at once. My business is an innovation-driven business, so this has worked for me.

*But* it can – and does – easily leak over into too much open loopdom, and I can get overwhelmed and exhausted. Plus, while I'm buzzing around having 10 big life-changing ideas, I frequently forget that I've turned the stove on to boil an egg, and I burn the pan. Pan after pan. Seriously. Just ask my husband.

My disinclination to close loops can be my downfall in other ways, too – when I'm gardening, for example, I love to plant seeds – but I hate harvesting. Weird, but true! I find closing loops really *boring* and hard work.

Since my loop revelation, however, I've realized that my next discipline is learning to close loops. Don't just take the peanut butter out of the fridge – put it away as well. Don't just start a million books – finish them too. I hate it! But I know that this is my growing edge – it's where I need to lean in.

Interestingly, my daughter Elly is the other way around – innovation isn't her thing, but she loves to close loops. She's very tidy, leaves her desk immaculate, gets pleasure from making sure that everything is just so. This, I think, is part of what makes us such a great team in the Chuckling Goat office: I open loops, and she helps me close them. I love having everything out where I can see it. And so, you see, I understand your kitchen table. Mine was much the same. Here's the thing, though – there's a sweet spot between having enough open loops to make you feel alive and having so many that you become overwhelmed. Your task is to find that sweet spot for yourself. I'm guessing that you need to lean in to the discipline of closing some loops to get there.

## Get rid of clutter that absorbs psychic energy.

And I can tell you right now, that all that stuff on your kitchen table represents *old loops that you must close before you move forward*. So, go on now – go clear that table, put out the flowers, make yourself a nice cup of tea and pick this book back up when it's nice and tidy! Oh, and take a picture before and after – if you get inspired, you can post the before and afters on our FB group, where we'll cheer you on! We've all been there.

It's super-important to know what kind of person you are. Are you a loop closer by nature, or a loop opener? Do you lean towards opening loops, or closing them? Which is easier?

Which is harder? Where do you need to lean in? Have a think about it, because I'm going to ask you to write about it in your very next step, which is...

# Step 2

# CREATE A BEAUTIFUL
# MORNING ROUTINE

**Ravish your senses to gain productivity. Make it
delicious! How to find an extra hour in your day.**

isten: no one – but no one – hates getting out of bed more
than I do. I'm a girl who can sleep for Wales. Me and my
duvet – we're a winning combination. However, it's occurred
to me lately that if I want stability and serenity in my life, I'm
going to have to put them there myself.

Unfortunately, no one is going to attend to this little detail for
me. And despite looking, I haven't been able to order them
online. Some things Google just doesn't have the answer for.

If you want to start your own business, you're just going to
have to make more time in your day. Think about it – you know
it's true. You're already running at top speed. How are you
going to fit a new business into that?

You're going to do it by creating more time. And you create
time in two ways:

1. Set your alarm for one hour earlier in the morning than you do right now and…

2. Go to sleep one hour earlier than you do right now.

You can do this. You really can. And you really should. Here's why:

## The time that you're spending staying up late at night isn't productive time, even if you think it is.

Chances are that you're on your phone, on social media or watching telly until you go to sleep. Yes?

All of those things disrupt your natural sleep patterns, which drains your vital energy – and none of them further the valuable contribution you're going to make to the world. So you need to trim the night-time bit back by an hour – and apply that extra hour to your morning, when you're fresh and clear and ready to do some valuable shizzle.

This shift is also good for your health, by the way. In Ayurvedic medicine, which is one of the world's oldest healing systems, they consider elements like lifestyle, diet and exercise to be crucial parts of well-being. Wacky, right? Or, maybe not so crazy, after all…

In any case, it does work – and regulating your sleep habits is good for your gut microbiome, which is the microbial population living in your intestine. In a perfect world, health-wise, you'd go to sleep at 10 p.m. and wake up at 6 a.m. I know – I don't do it either! But I get as close as I can. That's the goal.

Start going to bed an hour earlier and getting up an hour earlier, and in about three weeks you'll be amazed to notice how much more energy you have.

But there's one more thing you need to do to shore up your determination in those early days, when you're still dragging yourself up out of bed, cursing my name and wondering why you decided to do this.

You need to create a beautiful morning ritual. There are things you can outsource, and there are things you can hire other people to do for you. But creating a serene and stable workspace – and headspace – isn't one of them. Girlfriend, if you don't do this one for yourself, ain't nobody going to do it for you.

## Start the day on your own terms

The world is full of chaos and noise. And to get out in front of it, you're going to have to find a new gear. You're going to have to find more time in your day. You're going to have to work smarter, faster and with more focus.

Personally, I've found that the best way to achieve stability and serenity is by developing a delicious early-morning routine. I need to get out of bed early enough that I can control my day – at least for a while – before my day starts to control me.

It's all about acting with intention. Let's face it, the minute you get into the hurly-burly of the world, you're going to be dragged every which way. The phone will ring, the children will shout, the microwave will ping, the clock will march. It's going to be a rush and a palaver once the day gets going – we all know that.

So I get up early enough every morning that I show up for myself, first, before the demands of the day begin.

## In the early morning, I can decide what happens.

I have an essential oil burner in my study. The first thing I do is light the candle, fill the bowl with fresh water and drop some rosemary essential oil into it. I've become addicted to this scent. It's fresh, clean and actually has brain-boosting properties, according to science. And it smells lush.

I flip open my computer but – *importantly* – I don't check my emails. Don't do it! That's the outside world coming to get you. There will be time later to check your emails but this time is just for you. I go straight to YouTube, and put on the chants of Hildegard von Bingen, a mediaeval abbess. I do some yoga, because it's important to me that I do some intentional movement, that stretches me out to my limit. I meditate, because it's important to me that I practise intentional stillness, to quiet my crazy brain.

## Write your Morning Pages

And I journal. Boy, do I journal. Personally, I journal in a green extra-large Moleskine notebook, which has a soft cover and lined pages. I write with a wooden fountain pen, that I dip into a bottle of steel-blue ink. Do these details matter? Of course they do. Everything matters. Because *passion is in the details*. Some mornings I'll be lured out of bed just by the sheer thought of that fountain pen, the ink gliding over the crisp white pages. Mmm.

I journal because it's important that I have a conversation with myself, before anyone else gets hold of me. I practise offering surrender to the larger universe and asking for guidance from whatever is running this show. (More on this process later!) Why do I do this? Because there's no one else to tell me what to do. And I surely don't count on my own tiny mind to come up with answers.

I want to invite in the larger dream. These days, that's my boss – that's where I get my marching orders. Sweet friend, if you don't develop an agenda for yourself, someone out there surely has one for you. So give yourself the gift of waking up an hour earlier – and spend that time in conversation with yourself.

## Let your senses guide you

How do you know what kind of routine to develop? Well, this process is organoleptic. That's one of my favourite fancy words, derived from my study of medical herbalism. It means that 'acting on, or involving the use of, the sense organs'.

We're not very good at organoleptic perception these days, as we tend to get all our information from men in white coats. But this is how cave people gathered their data, back in the day. Pick up a leaf. Crush it in your fingers. Smell it. Taste it. Eat a bit. Wait ten minutes. How do you feel? This is the process of gathering information from our sense organs. You have waaay more knowledge and information than you know, stored in your body. You just have to let it out – and then trust it!

Do whatever feels good – do whatever you want to practise with intention. These are my suggestions for waking up your senses:

- Light a candle or burn some essential oil that smells delicious. Rosemary boosts brain function, which is why it's my choice for mornings – but find something that delights *you*.

- Play some nice music on YouTube – but *don't* be tempted to check your emails – not until much later.

- Make yourself a hot drink – it's too early for coffee, so try some hot water and lemon, or a herbal blend that delights you.

- Do some kind of movement.

- Practise some kind of stillness.

- Write in a journal that you love, with a pen you adore.

Ravish your senses. We need to wake up every aspect of our body and get it all aligned and working on our side. What do you love? What will lure you out of bed? Let's face it, the appeal of a warm duvet is hard to resist. I've found that by creating a ritual that involves every sense – smell, touch, taste, sound and vision, my body retains a memory of it that draws me awake in the morning. I can taste the lemon water, I can smell the rosemary, I can imagine the black ink scrolling onto the page, and feel the remembered pleasure of my brain stretching, waking up, engaging with the new day. That will get me out of bed when nothing else will.

It's got to be yummy, or you won't stick with it.

**What do you love enough to get up early for? Give it to yourself. And then show up for yourself. Because you, sweet friend, are worth showing up for.**

This comes from having a beautiful morning ritual that you pursue every day. When I say beautiful, I mean just that. It needs to appeal to you personally. It needs to appeal to all of your senses. It must be delicious enough to pull you out of that nice warm duvet. Our senses drive our experience, and we generally aren't very skilful in making use of them to further our productivity. Which is silly, when you think about it. Your serenity is your responsibility.

### Pick a location for your morning ritual

A ritual is something that's performed over and over, until it becomes habit and second nature. Then it's easier to do it than not do it. You're going to put the power of your habit to work for you, rather than defaulting into negative habits that keep you back.

A ritual means you're going to return here every day and harness the power of habit. Your body is a big ol' mammal, and you're going to train it, just like one of Pavlov's dogs.

Where are you going to have your morning ritual? It needs to be clean, warm, quiet and pleasant. If that's your newly cleaned kitchen or dining table, that's great. Just make sure that you're down there before anyone else wakes up – this is *you* time. It's not about cartoons or making breakfast or doing anything other than getting really good at listening to that quiet little voice inside your head.

Lay everything you need out the night before, including the (comfy) clothes you're going to wear. If you have to scrabble around finding your journal, pen, etc, you'll just stay in bed instead. Trust me, I've been there.

Now, how are you going to get your senses involved? Remember, to make it delicious enough for you to want to pry yourself out of bed, you're going to need something yummy to appeal to each sensory organ.

### Aromatherapy for mind, body and spirit

So treat yourself to an essential oil burner or diffuser. Diffusers are simpler, but I quite like the ancient ritual of lighting a candle each morning, and tea lights are cheap. Now, what's your favourite scent? Make it a proper essential oil please, not a chemical perfume or fragrance – they can be harmful to your microbiome. You can get 10ml of a nice essential oil relatively inexpensively, and you'll be giving yourself an aromatherapy treatment at the same time.

Lavender is nice, but it's very relaxing and in the morning I want something a bit more energizing to boost me. Lemon is lovely if you like citrus. Peppermint has brain-boosting abilities. Basil and grapefruit are known for their cognitive boosting abilities. Take your pick!

## Let's talk about sound

You know how easy it is to create your own little world when you're wearing headphones. That's what you're going to do here. So pick your music with care. I love Hildegard: I find the female voices uplifting and there's not so much of a pattern in the music that I get distracted. But again, this is about what's perfect for *you*.

What music puts you in the right frame of mind? You're looking to create a state that allows you to hear the quiet voice inside your head.

## Work with beautiful things

How about touch? That's your journal and pen. Now we all know, deep in our hearts, that starting one's own business is really just an excuse to buy some excellent stationery supplies! Ah, is there anything so exciting as wandering around a really good office supply shop or stationery store? So here's an easy assignment for you: I want you to buy yourself a brand new blank book. See, even though I'm asking you to wake up earlier, I'm on your side really.

Now this doesn't necessarily mean one of those beautiful hand-tooled leather jobs with the wrap-around bark button – although those are very lovely – but sometimes a blank book can be so nice that it's intimidating, and this book can't be that.

It must be something that you're willing to use every day and write things in that may be complete rubbish. For me, it's a willow-green, hardback Moleskine notebook, A4 size because my writing is huge and messy. To go with that, I've got a wooden fountain pen made for me by my brother-in-law, from a piece of laburnum he cut down on our farm. I use it with steel-blue real ink, in a glass bottle. Trust me when I say that if there was a fire, that fountain pen would be the first thing I'd go for. Every time I use it, I have the happy illusion that my lifestyle is finally – after five decades on the planet – coming together. The sensation doesn't last long, mind – but it's great while it lasts!

Full disclosure – I'm a bit of a Moleskine junkie. And no, they don't pay me for saying that. I wish. I've got a black one for the office, a green one for private journal, a blue one for client notes and a bunch of red ones for classes I take, when I'm learning something new (which I try to do constantly!). But that's me.

## What's your notebook and writing implement of choice?

It could be a pink quilted satin notebook and a peacock feather quill, with turquoise ink. I don't know. But *you should*. It's important. What's your taste? What works for you? Where do you want to sit? What kind of tea do you want to drink? Or is it coffee? Or a martini? How's the lighting? Pencil or pen? Computer or paper? Everything matters. Make these small choices with complete awareness, sensing your own likes and dislikes with exquisite discrimination.

Now if you're a hard-core business type, you may be sitting there rolling your eyes at all this soft stuff, waiting for the real discussion about business plans to kick in. (Don't hold your breath – I don't *do* business plans. Never have. Turns out, you don't need them!) But here's the thing:

You're about to start your own business. Your *own* business. No one else's. You're the boss. The wonderful thing – and the terrifying thing – about this process is that there's *no one to tell you what to do*. You need to start paying attention to that tiny internal voice that says, 'No – not that one – this one. Not the blue one – the green one.'

Passion is in the details. Everything matters. You need to be excited about this project in order for that momentum to last. This is a marathon, not a sprint. You must get familiar with the sensation of going, 'Oooh, I love *that!*' That's the feeling that's going to make you get up early and stay up late. Nurturing your own passion, imagination and creativity means making things delicious for yourself. If you don't, no one else will.

## Foster your little passions – they'll sustain the momentum of your journey.

Think of those points of passion as little will o' the wisps, that lead you to your destination. You don't know where you're going yet – and you don't have to. Just find the things that are lit up for you, and follow them, one at a time.

Passion doesn't come from generic things. It comes from the specificity of exact details. Does the feel of crisp white paper send you, or is it the blank screen of a laptop? Are you an android person, or a Mac? Do you write with a pen or a pencil? Do you sketch when you write, or are you words only? If you sketch, what do you use – water-soluble Caran d'Ache pencils, or bold crayons? Calligraphy pen or ballpoint? Rollerball or Sharpie? I can't answer those questions for you – only you can. You must start feeling your way into the details that get you excited, because they'll be very, very specific.

That specificity is what fires your imagination. And imagination is how the universe talks to us. That's the voice you need to listen to. Because that voice is your guidance system. That voice is your friend, your instructor and your director.

And the best way to start hearing that voice is to write.

## Choose your morning beverage

So we've got touch and sight covered (our journal and pen), smell (essential oil), sound (music)… What about taste? It's not a morning ritual without something to drink. So in those early moments when you stumble out of bed, head down to the kitchen and switch on the kettle and make yourself something delicious. Not coffee, by the way – first thing in the morning your cortisol level rises naturally. If you drink coffee on top of that action, you'll create a caffeine addiction. Wait for the time that your cortisol levels slump, like around 11 a.m. and after lunch. Then use it for that much needed boost.

Your morning beverage needs to be something a bit gentler; something that you love and look forward to. Ginger tea, maybe. For myself, I love a special brew we formulated at Chuckling Goat; Get Me Through the Day tea, which has rosemary, vervain, peppermint and mugwort. (Can you tell I love rosemary? Brilliant herb!)

•••••

Now you're ready to go. Music on, essential oil fragrance wafting through the air, delicious cuppa in hand. What do you write?

The exercises in this book will give you a starting point. By the time you've worked your way through the entire book, you'll be ready to branch out and freestyle. I always begin by writing down the previous night's dreams, if I remember them. Then I go on to do a bit of automatic writing – just apply your pen to the page and away you go, without regard for grammar, punctuation or logic, for three pages.

The relief of this is extraordinary. You'll find after a few days of feeling silly that it's like purging the murk out of your head. You'll write down stupid things, ridiculous things, emotional things, gripey-whiney things – and then suddenly, like hitting a wellspring of clear water, the ideas will start to flow. You'll be writing what you need to do that day, and why. You'll remind yourself of things that you'd forgotten. Important projects that you'd pushed to the back of your mind will resurface. (I always keep my to-do list next to my journal, for just that purpose.)

> **You're in dialogue with the universe, and it's where your best ideas will come from.**

A few weeks of following this practice faithfully and, I promise you, you'll be unable to remember how it was before – and unwilling to go back.

## Get physical and then focus

After I finish my journaling, I do a bit of physical exercise – on the cross trainer and then a few yoga stretches. Do what feels right for you. But I'd suggest you fit a few minutes – just 10 or so – of stretching and breathing into your morning routine. Your body needs to carry you through your day – wake it up and be kind to it.

And then I sit and meditate for five minutes. It's not a lot, I know, it probably should be more. But if I keep it to five minutes, I know that I'll do it every day.

I'm not a natural meditator. I don't like sitting still, and it's taken me ages to get to the point where I was ready to commit to doing it daily. But I do it now, in a specific pattern. I'll take you through my meditation in Step 13: How to Make the Right Decision Every Time.

## In a nutshell, when I meditate I align with my heart, and I align my heart with the heart of the world.

I ask for guidance, and I offer surrender. I listen. I commit myself to being heart-led through the day. And that creates a secure base for me. Then I get up and move out into the world, operating from that base. Ready to rock.

Hopefully, when we were children, our parents created a secure base for us. As business leaders, it's our job to *create a secure base for ourselves*. Sounds a little airy-fairy, maybe... but trust me when I tell you that it's not. Because when I walk into our full team meeting at 8 a.m. sharp, and meet the eyes of the crowd of people who now work for me, I need to be on top form. I've got to tell all those waiting faces how they're going to spend the next eight hours of their lives – and why it matters. It's up to me to inspire them, to lead them, to align them and to show them how to be part of something larger than themselves.

*Something worthwhile.*

I need to know what my own priorities are, because they're about to be assailed by every email in my inbox. I need to be in firm command of my own heart-led agenda. That's what my morning routine does for me.

## Either set your own agenda – or somebody else will set it for you.

If you don't have an agenda for yourself, the world is full of people who will damn sure have an agenda for you.

*Your serenity is your responsibility.* No one will develop it for you. No one will carve out space for you, roll out your yoga mat, write down your dreams and desires. No one will plan your day or give you the support you need to get started. That person is you.

So how are you going to support yourself today?

## *Step 3*

# START LIVING YOUR BEST LIFE NOW

There's no time to waste. You want to start living by your own values now. But... what are they exactly? Here's how to figure it out. Value-based scheduling.

I'm guessing that you picked up this book because you want to change your life. Maybe you want to leave your current job and start doing something that means more to you. Maybe you want to contribute something to the world. Maybe you want to create a life in which you have more time to spend with your family. But whatever the motivation, you want to change things, right? You're ready to take a journey.

I have some good news for you. The good news is that you can start living in alignment with your own values today – right now, after you do the following exercise. You don't have to wait until you make your first million or open your own office.

But before you begin a journey, you need to know where you're headed. So why is it that you want to start your own business? How will you know when you've succeeded?

What does it really mean for you to succeed?

Does it just mean to make a lot of money? According to the research, just making a lot of money isn't going to make you happy. If you don't believe me, just ask any of the lottery winners who ended up miserable and wishing that they had never won the stupid money in the first place.

I think we've failed to examine our terms carefully when it comes to success. I've come to believe that success has to do with succession.

## Lessons from nature

In nature, one thing succeeds another. Things happen in a certain inevitable order, in an unvarying pattern, moving forward with a certain grace. Summer succeeds spring, and autumn succeeds summer. In an ecosystem, the pioneer 'weed' species come in first, and they're then succeeded by other species. Any area if left untouched long enough will mature into a forest. That's succession.

We human beings aren't very good at this. We like to freeze things in a state of immaturity. We spend a lot of time and energy keeping our gardens as grass and flowers – according to nature, that's a state of immaturity, and nature is constantly and desperately trying to ensure that patch succeeds into a woodland. We fight back against this inevitable natural process with our chemicals and a whole lot of effort. As any gardener will tell you – relax for a moment, and nature will take over, with weeds and then bushes and then trees, until it's a woodland again. I personally love permaculture, which works with this process, instead of trying to fight it.

In the same way we human beings also try to freeze ourselves into a state of immaturity – just have a look at all the plastic surgery queens in the media.

I'd like to suggest a new model – that in human life, as in nature, one stage naturally succeeds another. For a woman, the fizzy, sexy stage of youth is like the spring season of a flower when pollen is on offer. Ideally, after pollination occurs, this early stage will be succeeded by maturity.

> **Your early sexy stage will be succeeded by another phase – where you wield wisdom, power and authority instead of youthful girlishness.**

And for some, this stage of mature authority will be succeeded by a stage as an elder where you're no longer in charge, but are instead cared for by others. This is natural succession.

In traditional tribal culture, tribes that included menopausal women out-survived tribes that didn't. That's why, it's reckoned, only human beings and whales go through menopause – because wise women who are past the child-bearing age are of such benefit to the tribe that it improves the entire tribe's ability to survive. So if you're a menopausal woman – congratulations! It's a great time to start a business!

Whatever your age or gender, any time in your life is a great time to start your own business. It's never too early or too late to begin this process.

But how do you know if you're succeeding? Success comes when you're living a life according to your own values. Not my values, or society's values – but your very own values. The ones that matter to you.

## Success happens when you're living a life according to your own values.

You need to know what you want, and what you value. Remember, if you don't have an agenda for yourself, there's a whole lot of people out there who will have one for you. And I can promise you this – if you don't know what you want, then you definitely won't get it!

But how do you know what you want? How do you know what your values actually are? If someone just walks up to you on the street and says, 'Hey, what are your values?', it's surprisingly difficult to come up with them. We tend to stammer and twitch and say, 'Well, you know… good stuff. Like family and – just having – a good life.'

We need to be more specific than that. But don't worry – I've got a fun little exercise for you that will help you figure out exactly what your values are.

### Schedule your true values into your everyday life

Get your journal and pen handy, and put them aside for now. Read these instructions through, and then lean back, close your eyes and take yourself through this journey of the imagination. When you're finished visualizing the whole thing, you're going to open your eyes and write down what you remember.

### Task 1: Look into the future and 'live' your best possible life

I'd like you to imagine that you're stepping into a time machine, which is whooshing you five years into the future. This future life is your own best possible life – your aspirational life – the one you want to have someday, in which you're running your own fabulously successful business and living your own marvellously satisfying life. There are no limits on this life, and it doesn't have to be connected to your current life in any way, shape or form. It could take place on Mars, or under the sea. No limits!

Now, in your aspirational virtual world, imagine that you're just opening your eyes, and it's first thing in the morning. You're waking up on a Tuesday – not a holiday, but a regular workday in your best possible life. So start by summoning up the sights you'd encounter as you prepare for just another day in your best possible life…

- Look around you – you're in your bedroom. What does it look like? What can you see? What are the furnishings like? The bed linens? Look over – is there someone next to you, or are you alone? If there's someone there, who is it?

- Now you're getting out of bed and walking over to the window. When you look out, what do you see? Walk over to the place where you keep your clothes and fling open the door. Pull out what you're going to wear that day. What kind of clothes are you putting on? What kind of shoes? Are they for indoor work or outdoor work?

- Now go to the area where you eat. Who's there, when you walk in? What kind of food are you eating? What happens while you eat?

- Now you're going to the location where you do your day's work. How long does it take you to get there? What mode of transport do you use? Do you see anyone else on the way?

- You're now arriving at your work location, wherever that might be. Walk in. Who do you see? Are there people there, or do you work alone? What does your work environment look like? Sound like? Feel like? What colours, scents and textures are there?

- Lunchtime now – do you eat alone? With people? Where do you take your midday meal? What are you eating?

- Now another chunk of work – are you doing the same thing, or something different? Are you working with your brain, your hands, both?

- Time now to head for home. How do you get there? How far away is it? Do you travel with someone, or alone?

- You walk into your living space again. Who is there? People, or are you on your own? What do you do before supper?

- Time for food – see the food, smell it. Look around the table. Who's there? What's the conversation about?

- Now there's a chunk of time before bed – where do you spend that? With whom? Where are you? What's going on around you?

- Time for bed – and it's the end of your day in your best life. Take a moment to breathe in the feeling of that aspirational day. Retain the colours, sensations, the feel of what it was like.

Now, open your eyes and jot down in your journal everything you can remember about your best possible day. What surprised you? What did you see that you didn't expect? What does it make you realize?

### Task 2: Find out the values that really drive your ambitions

When you've finished, have a look through what you've jotted down, and pull out the value drivers behind each entry.

**A value driver is what lies at the heart of any given activity.**

I want you to imagine that you're squeezing your best day like an orange and extracting the juice from each activity that you saw in your mind's eye. That juice is the value driver behind your imagining.

For example, if I imagine having breakfast with my family, the value driver there is 'connection with family', and if it's healthy food, the value driver is 'good nutrition'. If I imagine exercising, the value driver might be 'fitness'. If I imagine taking a walk on the beach, the value driver might be 'connection with nature'.

So extract as many value drivers as you can pull out of your imagined best day. They might be things like connection with friends, material success, creativity, personal development, rest, contribution, etc.

Write down these value drivers in their own special list. They're super-important!

## Task 3: Look at how you live your life today

Now, I'd like to come back into the present and think about a regular Tuesday in your current life. On a fresh sheet of paper, write down in your journal each of the fixed points in your schedule that occur on any given Tuesday. These are the marks that you must hit in order to fulfil your current commitments.

These fixed points might be different for each day, and different again on a weekend – but let's just concentrate on Tuesdays for the moment. Instead of thinking about this as a to-do list, think of it as a web that you re-spin every day – flexible and adjustable – and your fixed points as the landing points that you must hook to.

For example, do you have to cook breakfast for the kids? Walk the dog? Be at work by 8 a.m.? Take the kids to school by 9 a.m.? Pick them up at 3:30 p.m.? Soccer practice at 5:30 p.m.? Write down all the fixed points – or activities – to which you're currently committed.

## Task 4: Compare your current life with your value drivers

Now I'd like you to go back through your current schedule. Where an item on your schedule satisfies a value driver from your list, you can tick that value driver off. For example, if you spend time with the kids after school, and you have 'family connection' on your value driver list, you can tick off 'family connection'. There's something in your current schedule that satisfies that value driver – you're touching your value on a daily basis – so cross it off.

Continue on until you've cross-checked every item on your current schedule with a value driver.

Now go through and *circle* all the value drivers that are *not* being addressed in your current daily schedule.

These are all the things that you value, for which you're not currently making time.

Does it surprise you? People are often surprised when they see the ways in which their current everyday life isn't aligned with the things they value. In fact, often it's exactly 180 degrees opposite. Lots of people are spending most of their time on things they value the least – and failing to dedicate time to the things they value most. Here's the thing – your best life five years from now won't just happen. No one is going to wave a magic wand, and abruptly change everything for you. Change is a result of shifting one small habit at a time. And living your best life is something that you alone can create, one baby step after another.

But don't panic, because we're going to start making those changes today!

### Task 5: Start incorporating your values into your life now

Now I'd like you to go back through and pick up each circled value driver on your list – these are the values that you're not currently touching in your daily schedule. One at a time, look at your current schedule, to see where you could fit that value into your daily life. Look for the blank spaces, the holes, the places where you could stretch an activity to touch more than one value at a time.

## Stack your functions – and save time

At this point, I'd like to introduce the concept of stackable functions. This is an idea that comes from the study of permaculture. In a natural ecosystem, every element performs more than one function. A tree for example, doesn't just look pretty. It can also provide shade, shelter wildlife, produce mulch, act as a windbreak, raise the water table, fertilize the soil, prevent erosion, purify the air, and so on.

You're short on time, so every element in your schedule needs to serve more than one function, just as every element performs more than one function in a natural ecosystem. This is what enables the value-based scheduling to work.

If you have values of fitness and reconnection with nature, for example, you can touch both of those values by committing to take a walk outside every day, no matter what the weather. Value social connection as well? Great, arrange to do it with a friend. That's three values stacked into one activity – super-stackable functions right there!

You're probably already doing a lot of things in your day that could have stackable value functions. If you're eating breakfast every day (value: 'good health') and you value family connection you can stack these functions.

What would it take to make that breakfast time a fun family activity? Can you wake up 15 minutes earlier so that it's not a mad panic in the morning, and you have time to enjoy it? Can you make the kids a cup of hot chocolate with real raw cacao powder as a treat? (Sweetened with gut-friendly 100 per cent pure stevia or powdered licorice root, not sugar, which is harmful to your gut bugs, please!) Can you get them to set out their clothes and bags the night before as a launching pad? Perhaps make them a wall chart where they get a star for each chore performed before they leave the house in the morning?

Make it a goal to have breakfast as a fun family time – and you not only stack your functions but create some lovely family memories as well. My nearly grown kids still remember their star charts and breakfast chores fondly. We'd set a goal of being able to 'drift' out of the house – not churn, or straggle or panic, but actually drift out the door on time, everyone clean, dressed and fed, dishes put away and the house ready for the day. I'm not saying we managed it every day – but we got pretty close, and it was a lot of fun!

You have to eat breakfast and get the chores done anyway – why not tweak the process so that it serves several functions and increases your daily dose of joy?

## Tweak your schedule and boost your daily dose of joy.

You may also find that there are places where you're already doing something and it just needs pushing that tiny bit further to become part of your best life. For example, Claire in our WATT group said that she had a value driver to cook better food. She discovered that she was already spending time cooking every night – and that if she set some preparation time aside on a Sunday to cook from scratch and then freeze in batches, she could eat the kind of aspirational food she actually craved during the week. Look for the places where you can dust off activities that you're already doing, and value-charge them. Could you walk your child to school? That would fulfil the value of family connection – and also fitness and nature. Make every regular activity a value-driver activity and you'll fill your life with meaning!

Go through your list of untouched values. Organize, prioritize and stack functions until you're touching each of your important values in at least one way, every day.

And that's it – now you *are* living life according to your values!

<blockquote>
As this system develops and grows over time, it will become increasingly powerful, and you'll become increasingly joyful.
</blockquote>

That's because this schedule will grow along a frame of your own personal values – like a vine climbs a tree. No point in climbing a ladder, getting to the top and finding out that it's against the wrong wall. Make sure that all of your everyday activities are aligned with the things that you value – each and every day.

### Putting value-based scheduling to the test

If you're wondering how practical it is to incorporate values into everyday life, here's a real-life example from my own life.

I'd just come up with the concept of value-based scheduling and was working to implement it for myself. This is from my journal, at the beginning of 2018:

## January 2018

It seems to me that I've been starting with the wrong end of the stick – the tasks. Whereas, what I really need to do is start out with the end in mind – the thing I want to end up with, and then create the tasks that will put those values into my life.

So, as it's New Year, I want to make a list of all the things that I want in my life in the coming year. How do I want this year to be different to last year? What are the things that are important to me, that will enrich my life? What matters to me? How will I know when I've succeeded?

Here are my value drivers, from imagining my best possible life:

- Connection with my husband, Rich
- Connection with my 14-year-old son, Benj
- Connection with children no longer living at home
- Connection with parents
- Connection with my team
- Connection with my clients
- Creativity
- Connection to nature
- Build my garden
- Study herbs

- Declutter

- Rest and relax

- Time for spirit

- Fitness

- Drive my business forward, develop new products, etc.

Now, what are the fixed points in my schedule right now – the marks I have to hit, in order to fulfil my current commitments? Rather than thinking of this as a column of to-do lists, I imagine it as a spider web that I'm spinning, with certain fixed anchor points. I have a Mon–Fri web, and then a Sat–Sun web.

My Mon–Fri web looks like this. The fixed points are:

- 6:30 a.m. Stretch and exercise

- 7:30 a.m. Breakfast with Benj and Rich

- 8 a.m. Team meeting

- 2 p.m. Consultation with client

- 4 15 p.m. Pick Benj up from the bus

- 6 p.m. Cook supper

- 6:30 p.m. Eat supper

The rest of my time is, fortunately for me, pretty free. I can organize my time as I choose, living and working on the farm.

So now I look back through my value drivers. A few of them I can cross off. My 'fitness' and 'time for spirit' are satisfied by my yoga and meditation session in the mornings. My 'team connection' is satisfied by our morning meeting – although I need to flesh this out a bit, it occurs to me: I need to schedule a managers' meeting, and some department meetings once a month, to get more connected conversations with my managers.

I speak in-depth to one client per day, so that satisfies my requirement for 'connecting with my clients'.

One thing I notice right away however, is this – I'm spending almost *no* regular daily time with my husband! Crazily, since we run the company together, live together and work together, you'd think that we see each other all the time. But the way it works out – we just don't.

So I grab my notebook and go into the lounge, where Rich is hanging out with Benj because it's half-term. (He does a better job of this than I do.) I ask him if he wants to start having lunch with me. Usually we just grab something separately as we cycle through the day. We do usually have breakfast together, and supper as a family. Sometimes he'll come in and ask me if I'm stopping for lunch, and I do if I can manage it. But it would be much nicer if having lunch together was our default, rather than otherwise.

He's surprised, but pleased. We agree.

We also agree to take Friday mornings off from work, and go together into our little local market town, to visit the farmer's market. We used to do this all the time when we were so broke that we couldn't afford to shop at the large supermarket – and it was great fun. We both miss it, we decide. And now that we're directors of our own company, we can afford to enjoy taking some time off together, dammit!

So that was fun. Hmm, back to check my value-driver list. What else have I got?

I can see that 'connection to nature' is on my list, and I really want that to happen more than just once a week, on Saturdays. My goal is to get out and take a walk every day, whatever the weather. Could I do this with Benj, after I pick him up from school? But the bus doesn't come until 4:15 p.m. and by the time he's changed his clothes, etc., it's 5 p.m., and in the winter that means it's dark. No good for sloshing around the fields on the farm.

So what if I leave work a bit early – say 3:30 p.m. – and take a walk before I go pick Benj up at 4:15 p.m. Then I can make him a snack and hear about his day.

Rest and relaxation? A brief, hot bath before supper calms my nerves and gets me ready for the evening.

And how about the chunk of time in the morning? I break it down this way:

- 8:30–9:30 a.m. Work in the office. I can get everyone going on their tasks for the day, check my emails and deal with anything urgent.

- 10–11 a.m. Creativity. This is my time to go into my private study, and work on whatever project is current. Peak, fresh, juicy time.

- 11 a.m.–noon. Back to the office to work.

- 12:30–1 p.m. Lunch with Rich, if he's available. If he's not, I'll eat on my own.

- 1–2 p.m. Private study – either herbs or Welsh language, both of which I'm learning. After lunch I'm slower, not feeling so creative. Ready to take in content, rather than put it out.

- 3–3:30 p.m. Back into the office to check in with everyone, solve any problems, wrap up last-minute emails.

- 3:30–4:10 p.m. Walk

- 4:15 p.m. Pick up Benj

- 5 p.m. Hot tub

- 6 p.m. Fix supper

- 6:30 p.m. Eat supper

- 7–8:30 p.m. Family time

- 8:30 p.m. Put Benj to bed

- 9–11 p.m. Spend time with Rich

I can talk to my mum on Sunday nights (I already do this anyhow) and spend time on Saturday decluttering the house and working on my garden.

Sounds good on paper – now let's see how it works!

---

Looking back now to assess and tweak (more on this Try-Assess-Tweak process later!) I can see that it actually worked pretty well. This kind of value-based prioritization has become second nature to me now, and I do it automatically. My garden is well under way; I've pursued my goals of learning more about medical herbs by signing up for classes in Ayurvedic medicine, and now I've completed three out of four courses in the past year. Rich and I go away regularly on mini-breaks.

How does value-based scheduling work on a daily basis? Well, by now we're lucky enough to have a beautiful grandchild – Macsen – and two more on the way! Recently Rich and I agreed to look after Macsen on a weekday while his mum was busy.

I had a lot to do, and a bunch of deadlines to meet that day, one for a major newspaper. But when Macsen came over, I shut down my laptop, got out the aprons, spread the flour and sugar out all over the farmhouse kitchen, and Macsen and I had a great – messy! – time making cookies. Did I miss some important deadlines? Sure, I did. Did I care? Not a bit.

I have no regrets because I've thought carefully about it, and I know that my own primary value driver is connecting with family, not making more money or publishing more articles. I'd consider it a rookie error to look back in years to come and have any regrets about spending too much time working instead of with family. Money doesn't have arms, and it can't hug you back!

But those are just my values. You need to figure out your own values.

> Once you know what your values are,
> you'll make the right choice every time.

## Strike a balance between business and family

This is always an interesting topic. As I mentioned earlier, my husband and I started our business with the desire to spend more time together. As the business grew, we braided that value into the company. Our company motto is 'Family First'.

This means that we extend this flexibility to our employees – if a child or family member is ill, we immediately encourage them to go and tend to the family, and we'll support them as much as we can. Committed family people make better employees

– in my opinion this isn't only solid emotional intelligence but good business sense as well.

Realistically, for me, this 'family first' motto means that Benj will come marching into the office, firmly shut my laptop and say, 'Mum – family first!'

Now, I'm not going to lie here and say that this isn't sometimes infuriating. Because honestly, I'm a recovering workaholic. There's nothing that I enjoy more than working. My business truly is at that intoxicating intersection of what I love, what I'm good at, what I get paid for and what the world needs – and there's nothing so delicious. If I pass my laptop on a 'day off', I'll slope over, just have to have a quick look – just one little email – and before you know it, there I am hours later, still happily working away.

And yet...

I know that no one ever lay on their deathbed wishing that they had spent more time at the office. I remind myself of this as I take a deep sigh (one more email… I just need to finish the…), paste a smile on my face, get up out of my office chair and go outside to play a round of four-square with my son.

### This is, I know, is the right decision for me to make, even if it's tough in the moment.

And once I'm out there, laughing and batting the ball back across the line, I'm so glad that I've made that call!

We've also been very fortunate in being able to bring members of our family into our business. As soon as we were able, we started hiring more family. That was a happy day for us, and for the business! We've got daughter Elly running the office and son-in-law Josh working as our production manager. Rich's brother Rhys divides his time between teaching physics at a nearby secondary school and working on the farm as our groundsman.

Our latest addition to the team is our eldest daughter, Ceris. She's a qualified teacher with a master's degree in play-based education, and we've brought her on board to design and run a Montessori 'forest school'-type nursery for children of employees here at Chuckling Goat. Ceris is currently pregnant for the second time and Elly is also pregnant – so we're preparing for the third generation of family to join us on the farm. If life gives you babies, I say, open a crèche!

Family is woven into the very fabric of what we do, every day. The advantage of running your own business is that you can create it to suit your own unique situation. So, if you're starting your own business, I encourage you to start with your family in mind. Design your work life around your loved ones – humans, children or animals – whoever they may be! How will this benefit them? How can you include them in the equation?

## Tailor your business to suit your needs

In my case, I quite simply relied on my children as a workforce – and it's been nothing but good for them.

Our daughter Phia, now aged 19, was milking goats and making soap when she was 14. Benj has his own Chuckling Goat uniform (we call it kit), and works every summer, from 8 a.m. to lunchtime. He earned £1 an hour when he was 11, and £2 when he was 12. Now that he's 14, he earns £3 an hour. We've decided that, every year, his pay will rise by a pound an hour, right up until he hits minimum wage.

This has made both Phia and Benj strong, resilient and practical. The practice of getting up, putting on company uniform and going to work with the rest of the family has been invaluable for both of them. They work to earn the money that they're given. It's value for the kids, and value for the business.

## The beauty of mums running their own business is that the business can be designed from the ground up, with family in mind.

When you're the boss, you decide when and where you work. Working from your kitchen table is a beautiful thing because it allows you the flexibility to include your family in everything you do.

Remember – your life is your business! And all parts of it need to be nurtured, so that you can live a life you'll be happy to look back on at the end of the day.

*Step* 4

# WHAT IS YOUR BUSINESS?

**Here's a tool to help you figure out exactly
what your business should be. Your own
personal Five Directions compass.**

Okay, so now you've got a nice clear table, set with flowers. You've got a beautiful morning ritual, and a journal to write in during that time. You're going to sleep and waking up earlier, so your energy levels are starting to come up. You know what your value drivers are, and how to fit them into your current life. What's next?

It's time to get serious about your business. What's it going to be?

You're starting a journey here – and it's your own personal journey. You definitely won't be travelling on highways and established roads! It's more of an off-road adventure, this one. Consider this – if you can see your path clearly ahead of you, it's not your path. That's the road that someone else has carved out. You'll only see your own path when you look back and see the footprints you've left behind. You're going to create your own path as you go, and it's going to be unique to you.

So, for any off-road adventure, you need a compass to tell you which direction you need to head. It will help you find your personal magnetic north, every time you feel lost. I'm going to help you design your own compass, which will guide you in the right direction so that you need never feel lost again.

But let's talk for a moment first about your destination.

## What's your ultimate goal?

If your goal is simply to make a bunch of money, regardless of the impact that has on your family, the environment and the world around you – put this book down right now and give it to someone who will appreciate it. It's not for you.

But if you're interested in walking your gift out into the world and leaving the world better than you found it (just as a proper off-road explorer would do!) then keep reading.

Another myth that we need to examine and explode before we set off is the belief that you've achieved success when you reach a state of constant leisure. I think we all carry around this concept in the back of our minds: that somehow success is about making so much money that you no longer need to work.

B*((*£%$.

You don't need to sit still in order to be happy. You need good work. You need to know that you stand for something.

> **Happiness in life isn't achieved by perfecting leisure, no matter how much the magazines have sold us that dream.**

Happiness is achieved by having a purpose that's larger than yourself and working towards it. We're creatures of achievement – we're not built to wander around aimlessly, or slouch on the sofa forever. We want to do something – create something – feel ourselves as an important part of something that's larger than ourselves, and worthwhile. The goal isn't to make so much money that you can sit around for evermore doing nothing. The goal is to find your work – happy, productive, engaging work that fills a higher purpose. No purpose, no happiness.

Whether or not we're sent to Earth to achieve a certain purpose is very much a matter of individual faith. But the sure and certain knowledge that you must have a purpose – and follow it faithfully – in order to be happy on Earth, is pretty self-evident. There's nothing worse than the feeling of pointlessness – as if you're going round in circles without meaning or direction. That lack of meaning leads directly to despair. Do not pass Go, do not collect £200.

## Why hard work can be fulfilling

It's not hard work that's depressing – hard work can be fun, challenging, exhilarating. There's nothing better than collapsing at the end of a long day with a glass of something nice and your partner, and saying, 'Phew, that was a tough one! Did we win?'

No, it's not the hard work that's the enemy of happiness. It's futility – the sense that nothing you're doing matters – that you're part of a large and faceless machine that's eating away at the world, rather than trying to mend it. I know, because I spent 15 years living in the city, working in media. Five years as a newspaper reporter, and 10 years as a radio talk-show host. I learned a lot from each pursuit, no question. But particularly in the radio job, I constantly felt frustrated. Surely, I thought, with such a big bully pulpit – over a million listeners a night – I could do some good in the world?

And I did try! Anti-guns, pro-redwood trees – I picked up different causes, offered to give a voice to politicians who I thought were trying to make a difference. But I never managed to accomplish anything. In the end it all just felt like a lot of smoke and mirrors – entertainment for the masses – and a huge waste of calories.

That's when I began to long for the texture of a real life – heavy, cold, hard, slow, stone, leather, cast iron – something older, more real somehow than the plastic box in which I sat broadcasting, night after night. Not long after that I moved to Wales and I found my purpose. It's to help people find natural healing solutions to problems the doctors can't fix.

## It's a sense of purpose that gets me up early and keeps me up late.

I feel invigorated and excited. I love the bite of a new idea. I love the platform that the ideas have created – it's now big and strong enough to float me, my husband and our entire family into a new way of life, a happier, more secure, more prosperous life.

So that's my purpose. What's yours?

## What will get you out of bed in the morning?

It needs to be big enough – and inspiring enough – to pull you forward. It needs to be compelling enough to get you out of bed an hour earlier each morning than you currently wake up because you're going to need that time to dream your new life into reality.

We're aspirational creatures, we humans. We like to stretch, to be fully engaged, to run on all eight cylinders. Your purpose will provide the map that will start you on your cross-country journey – because believe me, this process is going to take you waaay off the beaten track.

So now I'd like to explore an important phrase in more depth: heart-led business. What is a heart-led business? Why does it matter? And how do you discover the focus of your own heart-led business?

### A heart-led business is one that's good from the ground up.

It's good for the soil microbes – good for the plants – good for the trees – good for the animals – good for your customers – good for you – good for the planet. It conveys value, all the way up the food chain.

If it doesn't fulfil these requirements, then it's not a heart-led business. And I'd suggest that it's much too late in the day of our group evolution as humans to start anything *but* heart-led businesses.

There's simply no gain in beginning an enterprise that sucks the juice out of one part of the ecosystem, only to bestow it on another part. Do that long enough, and the entire ecosystem will crumble. Why? Because we're all connected.

If you don't believe me, just look outside, at the environment. Or inside the human body, at the development of antibiotic resistance. The health of any ecosystem is determined by its biodiversity. The Amazon rainforest needs a gazillion different organisms thriving in it, so that it's resilient to predators or disease. Your gut microbiome is the same. Our society is the same. Anything that purports to help the whole by damaging or killing off part of it is a poisoned chalice solution that's doomed to fail in the end – and take the entire system with it.

Everything is a fractal – a pattern that repeats from the smallest, most invisible level to the largest, most infinite level. Did you know that scientists believe that there are trillions of living micro-organisms inside your gut, just as they estimate there are trillions of stars in the observable universe? Cool, right?

Imagine for a moment that the living organisms inside your gut are the inhabitants – and you're the planet.

From the microscopic to the infinite, it's the same pattern, all the way up and down the scale, big or small. And the rules for engagement with any living creature – any living ecosystem – are the same, all the way up and down:

## Love it. Feed it. Don't poison it.

You might say this sounds naive – and I might even agree with you. How can this airy-fairy nonsense possibly be a legitimate way to do hard-headed business in the real hard-headed world?

Except... that my business, built on these very principles and developed over just five years, now brings in a clear profit of over a million pounds every year. We started out with no deep pockets, no business plan, no previous business experience.

## The first building blocks of your business

So how did we do it? We grew it like a crystal, from the very beginning – so that it was right at every level. Then our crystal expanded into an entire ice palace.

Beginnings are like crystals – all the molecules need to be in the right place, or the end shape will be distorted. If you're going to build an ice palace, all the crystals need to be in alignment, or it all goes horribly wrong. This is why the phase you're in – of *setting intentions* – is such an exciting phase. Build your business from the inside out.

> **Create and nurture one tiny, perfect idea – one exact crystal – and then let it grow and expand.**

Never cut corners. Never compromise. Make it beautiful and keep it beautiful.

This is also why the end doesn't *ever* justify the means. You can't get to a good place by doing bad things and compromising your values. Your values are the very diamond heart of your business.

## Demonstrate leadership based on your own values

Be heart-led, and you'll never go wrong. An example for you: our company motto is 'family first'. We finish our workday at 4 p.m. so that people can go home and be with their families. Cash isn't king with us. If a customer is abusive to one of my team members, I refund their money and tell them we no longer wish to do business with them. Boy, do they hate that! ;-)

To me, 'family first' means that I take care of my team the same way I take care of my children. No one bullies them or makes them unhappy – *not on my watch*. My daughter Elly runs the office – and a damn fine job she does of it too! I wouldn't stand by while someone verbally abuses my own daughter – why would I stand by while a customer abused someone else's child?

Profits are good and important and can be used to do useful things in the world – but cash is most definitely not king, and it certainly doesn't give anyone the right to behave badly or mistreat my employees.

So I never cut corners. I never compromise. On anything. And I suggest that you do the same – from the very beginning. Get your crystal right, and your ice palace will be right. Stand for something good and pure and walk it out into the world.

> I'm here to tell you that you don't have to compromise your values to be successful in business. You can do well by doing good.

What are we doing with all our profits? Well, Rich bought me a convertible and a hot tub. We built a beautiful conservatory onto our old stone farmhouse, in clear view of the kitchen table where we started the business just a few years ago. And we built houses for all of our children, so they could live near us. That was fun.

As for the rest of the money – we're starting a Chuckling Kids crèche and farm school for the children of our employees – because, hell, why should women have to choose between their children and their work? They should be able to pop in and see their children on their breaks, always feel confident that the children are being well looked after, and breastfeed their babies as long as they want to. Don't you agree? In fact, while I'm at it, I may well start a campaign to get more childcare facilities into workplaces everywhere.

## Think beyond your current goals – dream big!

And we're also running a campaign to get kefir into the hands of pregnant women – because pregnancy is the best time to break the autoimmune cycle and improve the health of the child from birth. We're funding science projects to learn more about the microbiome and human health. I'm working on creating the ultimate business hub for my group of women entrepreneurs – one that has wildlife walks, childcare, shared hot desks, an organic farm shop and an exercise room. Because – why not? We deserve it! My goal is to leave this world better than I found it.

How about you? What will you do, with the money that your heart-led business will produce? How will you leave the world better than you found it?

It's never too early to dream big dreams
like this – these are the dreams that will
lead you forward and give you energy.

Remember – it's not about you. It's not about being greedy, or manipulative, or bragging. It's about giving your gift to the world. It's your responsibility to advocate for your gift and walk that gift out into the world so that it can succeed – and you can do more good with the proceeds.

So that's your destination. You'll want to keep it clearly in mind as we turn our attention to creating one of the tools that you'll need for your journey.

## Create your own Five Directions compass

You need your own virtual compass to give you direction. Every time you come to a crossroads – every time you're called on to make a decision, and that will occur many times every day, when you're running your own business! – you're going to need to refer to your own personal compass.

The first decision, unless you already have it firmly in mind, is what your business actually *is*. With such a plethora of gifts and ideas (you see, I do know you...) what exactly will your business be? How do you decide where to focus?

Here's how you figure it out:

To get there, we're going to create a kind of Venn diagram. This is a useful tool that lays fields over one another and works with the overlap. If you think about it, this is the way that a telescope – or microscope – works. It uses multiple lenses to allow you to see something very small and close up – or very large and far away. It's the interaction of the multiple lenses with one another that gives you crystal clarity.

For a model, I like to use a Celtic knot called the Five Directions. It looks like this:

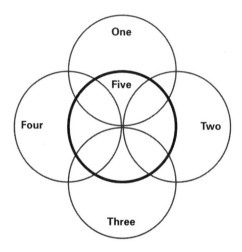

The Five Directions compass

Why Celtic? Well, I live in Wales, and I adore the poetry and the ancient history of these shapes. I love this shape so much that I even have it tattooed on my arm. You'll notice that this pattern has four interlocking circles – and a fifth circle that joins the other four together.

What does it mean, and how can it help you? Let's deconstruct it.

This shape is called the Five Directions knot. We start out with the Four Directions of the Compass. For this exercise I'd like you to get out five loose pages of paper – not simply pages in your journal because you're going to need to move these sheets around. But do get your journal ready as well because you're going to copy your final result into its pages. At the end of this, you're going to know what your heart-led business is.

Make these lists as full and long as possible – more is better. Write quickly and lightly, jotting down as many things as you can. Don't worry if things crop up on more than one list – in fact, as you'll see later, that's a good thing! Let those replications happen.

We start with the circle at the top…

## North

In the Celtic tradition, North is associated with the element of Earth – it means security, grounding, refuge, stability. It also represents the new Moon, solitude, darkness – more about that later, as we're going to use it in our lunar workflow! North also stands for order in law. But for the purposes of our personal compass, North represents money. We all need it to live, and there's no point in pretending otherwise. A business makes money – otherwise it's a hobby! So, on a sheet of loose paper right now, draw a big circle that represents the North. Inside that circle, I'd like you to write a list *all of the things you can already do that can earn you money*.

## South

Now we move to the South circle. In the Celtic tradition, South is the direction of fire and transformation. It represents passion, connection, social interaction, clarity in light. In the lunar workflow, it's the full Moon. So draw your South circle on a fresh sheet of loose paper now. Draw a big circle – there are going to be a lot of things on this list! Inside this circle. I'd like you to write all the things about which you're passionate. Passion signifies strength and excellence – so this is about *all the things you're good at*. Write these things in your South circle.

## West

Now we move to the West, which signifies water in the Celtic tradition. It also represents the three-quarter Moon, and relates to your emotions and purity. It represents growth in love. So what are all the things you love? On a third sheet of paper, draw a big circle and write a list of *all the things you love*, inside your West circle.

## East

East signifies air, the colour white, new beginnings, dawn, the first quarter Moon in the lunar cycle. It represents vitality in life. It's all about mobilization, inspiration and the higher path. So the question here is one of inspiration and the larger world. What does the world need? Write a list of *what the world needs* in your East circle now, on a fourth piece of paper

Now we have all four directions for the material dimension. What you can get paid for, what you're good at, what you love and what the world needs. But the Celtic knot has one more circle – that's why it's called the *Five Directions* knot. That centre circle stands for the universe.

## Universe

The universe's plan for you is the wild card. This is whatever your unfolding path is, whatever rolls out in front of you. It stands for all the synchronicities, mad accidents, 'random' things that occur for no apparent reason, that push you into an entirely new solution or situation. You can't ever completely predict your path, because no matter how logical you are and how carefully you plan, you'll find your little boat carried to strange new islands by mysterious currents that you can't control. Don't worry – that's where the treasure is! Don't fight that mysterious current – embrace it. Lean in to it. Listen for its quiet voice. Pledge to honour and take direction from it.

So draw your universe circle now and write down inside it all the strange coincidences or occurrences, things that you've noticed or seen or dreamed, books or phrases that keep cropping up, as if wanting you to notice them. These markers are pointers to *the universe's plan for you*. Write them all down now. If you haven't noticed anything, just leave it empty. There's great power in creating an empty category – it will get filled in time!

## The intersections hold the answers

Now this is the fun part. You've created five different circles – five different lists. Think of these five circles as five different optic lenses. I'd like you now to bring them together and look for the place where those lists *intersect*. These intersections may yield a lot of information for you along the way.

For example, take your North and South circles. Put the North circle on top, and the South circle underneath and look at these lists together. Where do they intersect? Which things crop up on both pages? This is the overlap between what you can get paid for, and what you're good at. This might well be your profession. But it's not necessarily good for the world – and you don't necessarily love it. Stay too long in this sector, and you may end up drying out, devoid of passion and a sense of mission. This isn't your heart-led business.

Now look at your West and East circles together. This is what you love, and what the world needs. The intersection of these two circles might be your mission. It's aspirational, it's good for the world, you feel strongly about it – but it doesn't make money. It's your cause, maybe – but it's not your heart-led business. Remember, a business is something that makes money.

How about what you're good at (South), and what you love (West)? This sounds like your *hobby*. Good fun – and perfect for your leisure time. But it doesn't necessarily make money – nor is it necessarily what the world needs. So it's not your heart-led business either.

You get the picture. Your heart-led business is the intersection of those four qualities: what you're good at, what you can get paid for, what you love and what the world needs. Missing even one of these elements will leave out a crucial ingredient. So put all four lists on the table in front of you. Where do they intersect? Write down that intersection in your journal.

And then you're going to add that one final filter. Where is the universe pushing you? What do the signs, signals and synchronicities say? If you haven't started noticing them yet, don't worry. You will!

So have a look at what you've pulled out.

These are the elements of your heart-led business. If there are elements missing, don't worry – this is a work in progress.

How do they fit together? I don't know. You don't even need to know at the moment! It's not necessary to know all the answers. It's just necessary to ask the right question.

All you need to do is to ask the question:

## How do these elements fit together into my heart-led business?

Imagine that you're typing that question into a huge cosmic Google and pressing search. Then wait. Don't try to figure this out with your brain. Your brain is logical, and it's great for processing data. But it's not the best for making decisions or coming to big conclusions.

Resist the temptation to figure this out. Just press that send button and sit back and wait. It may take days – but the answer will occur to you. It might happen at 3 a.m. – or in the bathtub – or while you're on a walk. But occur it will. Be patient enough to allow that to occur.

## *Step* 5

# FLIP THE NEGATIVE BELIEF PANCAKE

---

**What's holding you back from getting your boots on the road? Is it a negative belief? Here's how to flip it on its head and make it work for you.**

---

I want to talk to you about change.

We have this idea that change is hard, change is difficult, change is excruciating, and will take a long time.

But I've got some good news for you, if you're looking to change your life and start a new business:

## Change can happen in a heartbeat.

Your life is actually lighter than air. You can alter it in a moment. What's holding you back?

I'm guessing that it's your beliefs.

## Your beliefs determine your reality

What are beliefs? A belief is a feeling of certainty about *what things mean*. It's an interpretation of past events, that you hold firmly in your mind. Beliefs are the stories you tell yourself about the meanings of events that have occurred in your life. And here's the thing: your beliefs are always true for you, because they create the reality in your life.

When you were a kid, did you ever play with Play-Doh, squishing it through an extruder with a hole shaped like a star or a flower? Remember how the Play-Doh emerged in a long tube, with that exact shape? The finished shape was determined by the shape of the frame.

It might seem non-profound – sorry – but Play-Doh had it right all along. Your beliefs are the frame. Reality is the soft squishy stuff. And the shape of your reality is determined by your beliefs. Change your beliefs – change your reality. It really is that easy!

Here's a story about two brothers, to illustrate the point.

One brother tells this story:

> *Because my mother was a drug addict, I had no choice – I started stealing when I was seven. By the time I was 12, I was in juvenile hall. From then I progressed on to harder drugs and bigger crimes. I ended up an addict like my mother, and now I've been in and out of jail so many times that I've lost track. My life is ruined. I never had a chance. Everything I went through in my life made me what I am today.*

Brother number two tells this story:

*Because my mother was a drug addict, I had no choice – I had to grow up quickly so that I could take care of my brothers and sisters. When I was seven years old I cleaned the house and cooked food for everyone when she was passed out or on the streets. By the time I was 12 years old I got a paper route and started earning money. I worked doubly hard in school, so that I could graduate faster and get a better job and pay for my mother's rehab. I went to university, graduated and today I'm a tenured professor at Harvard. Everything I went through in my life made me what I am today.*

One reality. One mother. Two brothers, two different beliefs – and two totally different outcomes. See?

Your beliefs determine your reality.

As you can see from the story of the two brothers, there are two kinds of beliefs: negative beliefs that hold you back, and positive or empowering beliefs that pull you forward. If you think about it for a moment, you can easily identify the positive beliefs that are carrying you forward. They're the things that underlie all the successes that you've achieved so far in your life.

For example, I have a belief that 'I can learn anything'. I truly believe that if any human being can learn something, I can learn it as well. I can find a book, or take a class, and acquire that skill, if I work at it for long enough. (Okay, let's be honest, it probably wouldn't apply to astrophysics. But who knows – I've never tried that yet!)

Wow, this a great belief. It's taken me all kinds of places and allowed me to take risks and do crazy things. I've jumped off a lot of professional cliffs and acquired the survival skills I needed on the way down. That belief has never failed me yet.

So please take a moment now and write in your journal a list of all the *positive beliefs that you hold about yourself*, which have allowed you to succeed. Make the list as long and comprehensive as possible.

**Those positive beliefs are powerful forces in your life and will push you forward into creating your own business.**

Now, how about the negative beliefs? These are the real crunchers – the things that will stop you from taking a shot at something you really want. These are sentences lurking in your unconscious mind that start like this:

- 'Because I'm a woman…'

- 'Because I'm too young…'

- 'Because I'm too old…'

- 'Because I don't have enough experience…'

- 'Because I don't know what I'm doing…'

- 'Because I'm not good enough, not smart enough, not talented at math, don't have a business degree…'

And so on, and so on… Just fill in the blanks! Your mind can generate a million reasons to stop you from moving forward.

And remember: a belief is a feeling of certainty about the way things are. Those negative beliefs feel to you like absolutely rock-solid reality.

I'd like you, right now, to write down a list of all your negative beliefs. Go into that nightmare closet. Swing that door wide open and confront all those creepy-crawly fears about how you're not good enough, smart enough, not the right height or the right colour or the right gender or the right age to succeed. Flush those little monsters right out onto the page of your journal. Light, air and sunshine are the best antiseptic for those fermenting fugglies.

## Unpack those negative beliefs about yourself

Now take a good, long look at the negative beliefs that are holding you back. And allow yourself to wonder – where did they come from?

Here's the thing about beliefs – a belief is like a suitcase. You carry it around, and it feels real and substantial. But you know when you check in for your flight at the airport, and they ask you if you packed your own bags?

Most of the time, we don't pack our own belief bags. Many of our beliefs about ourselves were put there by dismissive parents, or mean siblings, or Mrs Jones in second grade, who told us we couldn't sing.

So the question about your beliefs is: Did you pack your own bag?

## Where did these beliefs come from?

Were they packed for you by people you trust, admire and respect? Qualified experts who really know their stuff? Or did they come from your mother (bitter about her own failings), the bully on the corner (hated you for being smarter) or nasty old Mrs Jones (really should have retired 10 years earlier)?

Was Mrs Jones really qualified to tell you not to sing, that you should just mouth the words while everyone else in the chorus carried the melody? Or how about Mr Davis the art teacher, who criticized your drawing because horses aren't blue in real life? What belief went into your suitcase that day? And are you still not drawing, 30 years later, because of what Mr Davis said? Was he a trusted adviser? Was he really the kind of person whose word you'd take about your artistic abilities, if he was standing in front of you today, in his creepy checked polyester trousers?

You know what I mean. You have your own stories – your own Mrs Jones and Mr Davis. You have your own moments of pain, when people told you that you weren't good at this or that, and you believed them. So write all those beliefs down – along with the moment you started to believe them.

## Flip the 'belief pancake'

Now – it's pancake time. We're going to take some of those negative beliefs and *flip* them. How does this work? Here's an example:

When I was 26 years old and working as a newspaper reporter, I was contacted by a wonderful woman named Robin Bertolucci, who recruited talent for the biggest news talk radio station in the area. She liked my writing and thought I had radio potential.

'I think you'd make a great radio talk-show host,' she said. 'You should try it.'

I was appalled. Not to mention completely terrified. 'I can't do that!' I told her. 'I'm a woman, for one thing, and all the talk-show hosts are men. I'm way too young, and too inexperienced. I don't know anything about politics. I'm not an expert like all those commentators you have on the air, all those men with degrees in political science who know their civic history inside out.'

Do you hear all the negative beliefs there?

1.  Because I'm a woman, no one will listen to me.

2.  Because I'm too young, I'm not qualified.

3.  Because I'm not an expert, I'll lack credibility.

*Now wait for the negative belief flip, because here it comes...*

'It's because you're not an expert that I want you,' Robin told me. 'You can use that. You can say, "Look, I'm no expert, but here's how it seems to me." People will relate to you. You're young, and a woman – that makes your voice unique. Different. Interesting.'

She took all the limiting beliefs I had, and flipped them right over on their heads, turning them into assets instead of liabilities. Robin coached me intensively, and here's how my beliefs looked when she was done:

1.  Because I'm a woman, I have a unique point of view to offer – different to all the men currently on the air.

2.  Because I'm young, I can give the perspective of the younger generation.

3.  Because I'm not an expert, I can give a common-sense response that will resonate with a wider audience.

I trusted Robin – and she was right. I went on to have 10 successful years on the air as a radio talk-show host on the back of that pancake-flip.

If I could clone Robin and pass her around to everyone, I would. Everyone needs a coach to help them flip their negative beliefs over and turn them into assets. But you can do this process yourself. I want you right now to go back through your list of negative beliefs, and pancake-flip every one of them. Find how that belief can serve you. Turn that liability into an asset. Write down the new belief.

*'Because I have no previous business experience, I'll never succeed'* becomes…

*'Because I have no previous business experience, I can come at things from a fresh and unexpected perspective.'*

You can do this! Get flipping.

This pancake-flipping process is a gift that keeps on giving, by the way. It's a muscular discipline. Get good at this, and it will take you to places you never imagined.

Here's how it worked for me later on:

## The power of asking, 'What if...'

Many years after Robin showed such faith in me, my husband lay on the sofa, suffering from an antibiotic-resistant superbug infection. The doctor came to have a look at my husband's abdominal wound. It was riddled with little red holes full of flesh-eating MRSA that were burrowing closer to his vital organs every day. The doctor said, 'I'm sorry, I have no experience with anything of this magnitude.' He jumped in his car, *locked the car doors* and sped off up our farm track.

I remember very clearly feeling my knees give way and the blood drain out of my head. I remember thinking, 'Don't leave me here alone! I'm not a doctor! I don't have any training! I can't help him!'

And in that moment, Robin's voice came back into my head. I remember the way she'd flipped my negative beliefs on their heads. 'What if...' I thought. 'What if that's a negative belief that I could flip? Maybe... because I'm *not* a doctor, I can ask stupid questions doctors would never ask. Maybe because I'm *not* a doctor, I can look for answers that doctors wouldn't see. Maybe I can see things in a different way, try things doctors would never try.'

So I started researching antibiotic-resistant infections. (Remember my empowering belief – that I can learn anything? It came in handy here!) The main thing I noticed was how aggressive all the language was. It was all about 'fighting the bad bugs' and 'killing the harmful bacteria' and 'winning (or losing) the war against infection'.

It struck me that the entire frame was wrong. The whole debate was doomed to failure. You can never win that way. I'm not a doctor – and maybe because I'm not I could see that killing just creates more killing – never resolution or harmony. Clearly, we'll never get anywhere by trying to kill all the bacteria. There are just too many of them, and you can never kill them all off. In fact, what I started to notice was a bunch of negative beliefs with a recurring theme:

Old belief: 'Because the bacteria are our enemies, we must kill them all off.'

But I couldn't kill them all off. That's the point of a resistant superbug. Someone has already tried to kill it and failed – and that's what has created the ongoing problem. The 'resistants' have survived and bred, and now they can't be killed. So I pursue that line of reasoning to its end, and – I fail. My husband dies. No good: I don't like that result. Back to the drawing board.

So, I thought, how might I flip that belief? What's the opposite of killing? How about – dancing? Making friends? Creating alliances? Could I dance the bacteria into harmony, using microbiotic allies? Crazy, right? But here's how I flipped that belief:

## 'Because the bacteria are out of balance, we must bring them back into harmony using microbiotic allies.'

And you want to know something else that's crazy? *It worked.* Because, as it happened, it was true. I didn't need to kill the bad bacteria. I just needed allies on the microscopic level, to bring the ecosystem back into balance and put the pathogens back into their box inside the microbiome.

Using that frame, the answer was right in front of me – in the kefir that I was making on our kitchen table. I washed Rich down with an alternating combination of essential oils, to create a foothold, and kefir, to get the good bacteria back into the skin biome. It worked. Rich swabbed clear of MRSA after two weeks, got up out of bed and got on his tractor – where he remains to this day!

Result – I saved my husband's life. Secondary result – I learned how to use the kefir to bring the microbiome back into balance on the skin, as well as inside the gut. Next, I used my 'I can learn anything' belief again to learn how to make soaps and lotions, and I put the kefir in them. This combo created incredibly effective results for eczema, rosacea, psoriasis and other autoimmune skin conditions. Our business went stratospheric. Lovely happy ending, of course – although not half as important to me as saving Rich.

## Negative beliefs don't help anyone

Turns out, the belief held by the medical establishments that 'antibiotics are the answer to everything' – is a negative and limiting belief. It's a belief that's crippling Britain's flagship National Health Service and leading to serious problems in health systems across the developed world as terrifying superbugs evolve. In 2017, England's then chief medical officer Dame Sally Davies warned world leaders of a 'post-antibiotic apocalypse' in which a standard hip operation could become a life-threatening event due to the risk of superbug infection.

So let's look at the old negative and limiting attitude…

Old belief: Antibiotics = 'against life' = killing things, a poisoned-chalice solution.

...and flip it...

Flipped belief: Probiotics = 'beneficial for life' = a solution that boosts health by creating harmony.

Probiotics are the way forward, on every level, microscopic to social, to galactic. Less killing – more dancing things into harmony. Boost the good things, and they'll bring the harmful ones into line. Remember, it's a fractal all the way up and down. Whatever it is – love it. Feed it. Don't poison it.

Whatever the focus of your business, cleaning out your belief suitcase will make you lighter. You'll be able to move faster. It's not so hard to catch that success train that's leaving the station if you don't have to drag all those crippling, outdated negative beliefs around with you.

## Ditch the old negative beliefs that have been dragging you down.

So get flipping those negative beliefs like pancakes. Listen out for negative beliefs in your own language – in the language of people around you – in the conversations of the world community. Spot 'em, and flip 'em!

### Inner strength forged in crisis

Side note: This period of my life during Rich's illness was what I now call my 'crucible period'. It was a time of great stress and emergency, when everything I had was called into question. It was a time of enormous heat and pressure, and I wasn't sure I would – or could – come through it. But just like a real crucible, it melted everything down and refined it into something new. On the other side of that experience, I had knowledge and insight that I didn't have before – as well as a new focus and drive.

Many people that I know who run their own businesses have gone through a similar crucible period. It might be an illness – their own, or that of a loved one. It might be a bankruptcy, or a crisis; a move or a bereavement. If you've been through your own crucible time, you'll know exactly what I'm talking about.

## Crisis can purify you, refine you and leave you stronger on the other side.

Old belief: 'Because I've been through a difficult crucible time, I'm too damaged and dented to start my own business.'

Flipped belief: 'Because I've been through a difficult crucible time, I'm stronger, more focused and more prepared to succeed in my own business. I'm solid gold.'

Which negative beliefs can you flip onto their heads today?

## Assets, allies and attitude

There's a negative belief floating around out there that you need loads of resources before you start your business: deep pockets, an investor, lots of money. *Not true.* We started our business flat broke, with one goat and a sack of feed.

You can flip that belief over into an empowering one.

Old belief: 'Because I don't have a lot of financial resources, I can't afford to start my own business.'

Flipped belief: 'Because I don't have a lot of financial resources, I'm hungry enough, innovative enough and creative enough to make my business out of nothing – and it will be all the more satisfying when it succeeds!'

Your assets at the moment may not be financial. But that doesn't mean you lack assets. Perhaps you're just not counting the assets you do have.

At the centenary of the end of the First World War, I started thinking a lot about the pilots in that war. I was specifically fascinated by those brave people who were stranded – or jumped intentionally – behind enemy lines, to complete missions or try to survive until rescues could be accomplished. People back then seemed so much tougher than we are today, probably because they had to be. They did so much, with the little that they had.

I started thinking about the mindset those pilots must have had in order to survive behind enemy lines, and I wondered if it could be of any use to us today.

What must they have been thinking about? What would have controlled their focus? Imagine it – you'd have had to strip everything down to questions of immediate survival and bring your focus to a sharp point. As you landed, you'd already be gathering up the parachute and rolling out of the way. Scanning the environment for shelter. Looking for where you should move next.

If you're feeling stuck, try this exercise in your journal. What would happen if, in your imagination, you pulled yourself up out of your situation and then parachuted back into it, with the eyes and mind of a pilot intentionally going behind enemy lines.

I think they may have thought about three things:

1. Assets

2. Allies

3. Attitude

## Assets

What have you got on you? What do you have in your pockets? Shoelaces, a belt buckle – what can be used to help you? I wonder how often we really do a full count of all of our assets, with an eye to making every possible thing work for us. How amazed people of yesteryear would have been to look at our storehouses of food, friends, conveniences. What do you have that you're not making use of?

## Allies

Who's around you, who might help you? Where is there a friendly face? Who could offer you support, shelter, a meal, some protection? Where can you ask for assistance?

## Attitude

The most important one of all. What would you have had to think in order to stay alive? Not despairing thoughts. Not resentful thoughts. Not thoughts about how life is unfair or wondering 'Why me?' I doubt that anyone who strayed into those areas of self-pity would have made it through. They would have been focused, I guess, on moment-to-moment survival. On the next small increment of what could be done, what could be accomplished. A laser focus on what to do next, using all their forces of intuition and energy. Activating their entire being to move forward.

So go back and do a recount of the things on the plus side of your ledger. Get tough with yourself. What are the assets, allies and attitudes that you can deploy, to help you survive and thrive? You have more to work with than you know.

## *Step* 6

# TAKE YOUR FIRST STEPS

---

**There's a difference between dreaming about it – and actually doing it. Get the courage to move forward. Dirt is the flavour. How to put a price on your work. How to put your face on your business.**

---

One of my favourite phrases is: 'Put your boots on the road.' But what does this mean exactly?

It has to do with pushing away from something I call the 'fantasy curve'. Loads of people dream about doing something. It's incredibly seductive to have fantasies about what your business could be/should be, some day when you get it all perfect, and have it all together.

Fantasy has a different texture to reality. Fantasy is seamless and smooth, like plastic. Reality on the other hand is gritty, hard, cold, rough, broken. It's nothing like fantasy. If you've actually put your boots on the road, you know exactly what I'm talking about. The things that really happen are absolutely not what you'd expect them to be, and there's no way to anticipate them.

> Reality – and the universe – has a way of
> slinging you down another path entirely.

I ate this gritty cookie in its entirety when I came to the farm in the first place, as a city girl. Living on a goat farm by the sea? Sure. Lovely. I could see myself, dressed in something floaty and floral from Laura Ashley, with a wide-brimmed hat and a copper pail (Copper? Why copper? Copper is heavy and is never actually used to hold animal feed. But that's the fantasy curve for you), drifting down a sunny slope. I'm sure there were buttercups in the grass, and birds singing somewhere. A bit of a cross between Heidi and Snow White, now that I really get a good look at this fantasy down on paper. Notice that the goats aren't even *in* this picture! It's more about the floaty dress.

## Living the dream?

Well. I hardly need to tell you that real life on a farm is *nothing* like my fantasy curve. This came fully to my attention on the day that I was kneeling on the goat-poo-strewn barn floor on a freezing cold day, dressed in layers of army surplus fleece, rubber boots and waterproof trousers, rubbing down a newly born goat kid and spraying its umbilical cord with iodine. The mother goat, who had just given birth and was busily eating the afterbirth, swung around and slapped me full across the face with the entire sloppy, gloopy mess. I just wiped the afterbirth off with my sleeve and thought, 'Yup. This is really not how I imagined it.' Not a single Laura Ashley print in sight.

But there were other lessons I couldn't have imagined. I learned from watching the newborn goat kid slam its head into the mother's udder in order to make her let the milk down, that nature works in a call-and-response pattern. You ask, and then you receive. Being pummelled hard wouldn't work for me, as a human mother, but it works for the goats. I began looking for the appropriate call-and-response pattern all around me, and I found it everywhere on the farm. There's an action and then a reaction.

That piece of knowledge became deeply embedded in me. It taught me that everything is about engagement.

> ## It's a back-and-forth interaction, not just a one-sided broadcast.

And when I started interacting with my customers, I carried this knowledge with me. I focused on interaction, and engagement. I stayed in close contact with my customers, and when they asked for something, I provided it. I didn't launch a new product until my customers demanded it.

## Knowledge born of experience

This drove later decisions as well. We decided not to sell through outside retailers, because I needed to stay in close contact with my customers so that I could feel the back-and-forth interaction. Why would I pay a retailer 25 per cent of my profits to contact my customers? I want to contact my customers. I need to stay in close contact with my customers. This has completely shaped our business and our explosive growth. And I learned that from watching the goats. I learned it from the day-to-day reality of putting my boots on the road.

Now that's not something you're going to make up in your fantasy. Fantasy is a lot more superficial, and it doesn't have deep, hard-won knowledge in it. This kind of knowing is bone-deep, and it only comes from reality.

> You've got to be in it to win it. Get up off the sofa, pull your boots on, open the door and get out there, so the adventure can begin.

Doing a fantasy, armchair version of your business is never going to be enough. You'll never learn through a fantasy. You'll never grow, through a fantasy. The actual journey isn't going to be perfect, and in fact, it's probably not going to be anything like your fantasy. And that's a good thing.

## Don't wait for the 'right' time

Putting your boots on the road also means that you just take one step, and then another. And then see what happens. You don't have to have it all together before you begin. You don't have to be perfect or have all the skills in place. Get out there and tangle with the way things really are. The journey itself will teach you what you need to know.

So what are the nitty-gritty beginning pieces of putting your boots on the road?

Well, once you've done the work of figuring out the focus of your heart-led business – what product or service you're going to offer – you need to figure out what to charge for it! This is a process that brings all kinds of gremlins out of the nightmare closet. Let's examine those little critters in more detail. Like all scary nightmare closet-dwellers, it's best to give them a good dose of light, air and sunshine to shrink them down to manageable size.

## Putting a price on your work

So you've created your product or service. Now, how do you price it?

This is a difficult issue for a lot of women in our WATT group because it immediately gets tangled up with issues of self-worth. You may already be producing your product or service, and giving it away to people because you feel hesitant to charge actual money for it. After all, it's just *fill in the blank with your product or service*.

Beware of the word 'just'. It's an indicator that you're downplaying whatever it is that comes after it. 'Oh, I'll just pop over and tidy up after those 50 screaming children.' 'Just' is an indication that at some level, you know that you're looking at something significant – and you're already trying to talk yourself past it by downplaying its importance.

> ### Look, it's not 'just' anything. It's a wonderful thing, and you deserve to get paid for it.

In fact, I'd like you to write the following statement in bold, clear letters, and put it by the side of your bed. I want you to look at it in the morning when you first wake up, and at night before you go to bed.

It goes like this:

### I do wonderful work for wonderful pay.

There you go. That's it. Your wonderful work deserves wonderful pay. And furthermore, people won't value your product or service unless they pay for it.

## Have faith in your product

We have this issue with our kefir. It's expensive – £40 for a three-week course. I don't sell sample bottles. Why not? Because the kefir is a decision that you have to make. It doesn't taste particularly good – it's a fermented, unsweetened product. It's a therapeutic medical food, not a yummy milkshake. It's not supposed to taste good.

But as with all natural healing methods, kefir works slowly inside your system. One bottle won't produce results. You need to take it in a sustained way over time. People need to commit with their brain, not with their taste buds, and make a financial investment in their own long-term health. They need to walk through a commitment gateway. Then, once they've invested and received their kefir, they'll work harder to make themselves drink it, along with making dietary improvements. Often then they find that they quickly become accustomed to the sour taste and even begin to crave it.

But they must make the commitment to getting healthy first.

### And if they don't pay for it, they won't value it.

Pricing your product too low isn't a favour to your customers. Think about it for yourself – if something is extremely cheap, don't you wonder if it's actually any good? Whereas the face cream that sells for £200 per pot must be great because it's so expensive!

Advice point #1: set your price point high. If you start too high, you can reduce it in future by having a sale – but you can't substantially increase it once it's out there.

## How to set a price point

How do you know what to charge for your product or service?

Well, you start by figuring out how much it cost you to make. This is a tricky one, and it involves paper, pencil, a computer, lots of coffee and a free space of time when you're really fresh. Don't underestimate the amount of time this process takes, or the difficulty of it. It's complicated, but worthwhile. And you can't proceed without this information. So make an appointment with yourself on your calendar, sharpen your pencil and turn up.

First you must calculate a costing. A costing is how much it costs you to provide one unit of your product or service.

## Breaking it down

Let's take, for example, my Get Me Through the Day Tea. It's one of my favourite recipes, made from loose-leaf herbs. I made it up by request all the time for my team members, and finally just started selling it so that the girls in the soapery could make it instead of me! It gives you a great non-caffeinated boost to make it through those long, weary afternoons.

The ingredients are: rosemary, vervain, mugwort and peppermint. Rosemary and vervain for mood boost, peppermint for brain function, mugwort to kill off any potential cold bugs that might slow me down. Each bag contains 100 g of product, so that's one unit. If I was costing soap, I'd cost for one bar.

> ## So first I need to figure out how much the raw ingredients – in this case, herbs – cost me to buy in.

I can go on to an appropriate supplier website and price up each individual ingredient. I'll pick a standard order size – say, 1 kilo of product – then I can divide it down. How much does one kilo each of rosemary, vervain, peppermint and mugwort cost me? I make up the figures for 1 kilo, and then divide down until I come up with the cost of 1 bag of 100 g.

If you haven't yet settled on a supplier for all of your ingredients, don't worry – just use the Internet and pretend that you're ordering. Look up what you think you might use and get the prices that way.

## Containing the issue

The next thing to consider is the packaging. For all our teas we use brown paper bags, and we hand-stamp them with a rubber stamp. My designer has spent time designing the bags, and we've purchased the stamp – but I don't include those, because they're one-off start-up costs. It's only ongoing running costs that I'm adding in here.

So, I add in the cost of the bags. And the ink pads, because I'm going to have to continue to re-purchase those. How many bags can I stamp with one ink pad? Do the math, then add in the cost to stamp one bag. Tiny, maybe – but it all counts towards the total. And don't forget the cost of the stickers on the front and back.

## Keeping the lights on

While the tea is being mixed, the lights are on in our still room. That means I have to add in the cost of electricity. If the production process was using water, I'd add that in too. And yes, you're actually going to have to go and find an electricity bill, and figure out what you're spending on electricity per hour, how many items you can produce in one hour, divide the cost of an hour's worth of electricity by the number of products made in an hour, and add that figure in. How much does it cost in electricity to produce each single unit of product? Same with water. If you're working from home, figure that you can take half of your electric costs for business.

I told you it would take a lot of coffee! Stick with me though, it's worth it.

## Know your own worth

Now comes the killer. You're going to have to add in the cost of your own labour.

But I'm not paying myself! I can hear you protesting. I can't afford to pay myself yet!

I know, I know. But someday, when your business gets successful, you're going to hire someone to help you. And that's how you figure out what your time is worth.

## How much would you have to pay someone else to do the work that you're doing right now?

Now obviously, no one will ever do it as well as you're doing it yourself. No one will do it with the same care and passion. But you can, actually, I've discovered, hire a body to do almost anything in this world. So, how much would you have to pay them, per hour? Go ahead, figure it out. If you have no idea, go to indeed.co.uk – or an online job service that's local to you – and type in a similar job description. Pick an average salary – neither the highest nor the lowest. You may be amazed by how much your time is actually worth! Or, you might be surprised to see how cheaply you could hire an assistant.

In my case, I wouldn't include in the costing my innovation and research time when I was originally working out what herbs to put in the tea because that was a one-off. It's just the ongoing cost of someone actually mixing up and bagging the teas.

### *The bottom line*

Now you know how much your product costs you to make. This is really important because if you're charging less than it costs you, *it's a hobby, not a business.* Which is fine – but you just need to be clear about that.

A business makes money. That's why it's a business.

## *Scope out the marketplace*

Next step is to go and look at your competition. What else is out there? What similar products or services are on offer, and how much do they cost? This is an Internet job. It can be slightly sick-making, to spend time looking at your competition, but you absolutely must do it. Maybe take a break and have another cup of coffee to steel yourself.

You need to have an idea of the market you're entering. Write down a whole list. Low-, high-, medium-priced options. Now have a very thorough think about where you want to sit in that market.

**Are you the bargain variety? Or are you the posh deluxe version? Or are you the sensible mid-range option?**

Whichever you choose, you're going to need to stick to it – because you're going to need to communicate this information to your customer with your packaging and branding.

Think about your own shopping habits – with certain things, you look for the cheapest options. Others, you shop for the middle. And others – maybe – you treat yourself. Your customers are the same. So figure out where in the market you sit.

Set your price. And then increase it a bit. Because... you do wonderful work for wonderful pay!

## Put your face on your business

Part of putting your boots on the road is putting your face on your business. You're going to have to let your customers see you, whether it's at a table at a craft fair or putting your picture up on your website.

You may shrink from this prospect in horror. I know I certainly did. And I had a great get-out clause – I had the goats! Sure, I didn't have to put my face out there: I could put pictures of the goats – they're adorable, people love them! No one wants to see me!

## People buy from other people, not from anonymous businesses

Luckily for me, I had the advice of a great mentor, Janey Lee Grace of Janey Loves. Janey coaches heart-centred businesses, (if you haven't taken her training, I highly recommend it!) and she knows all the traps people fall into. She explained it to me simply – 'Customers buy from someone they like, know and trust. A person, not a goat. Put your face on your website, and they'll begin to like, know and trust you.'

Like a lot of creative people – maybe like you? – I'm actually pretty introverted. I don't particularly like to be the centre of attention. That's just not where I live.

However, I did this because it was in the service of my business. And Janey was right – it made all the difference. People want to know who you are. Sorry, there's no way around it. Your personal, unique story is what makes your business different, special… well, unique!

But here's the good news – you don't have to be perfect. In fact, you shouldn't try to be perfect. Instagram aside, that's not what people want to see. Think about it. If you're scrolling around on social media, what would you rather see? A story about someone who apparently just baked a pan of perfectly baked, faultless muffins? Or an honest, funny account of someone who put in too much baking powder and had to scrape the charred globs off the top of the stove, laughing at herself as she did so?

## You see, it's universal. People relate to your honest authentic stories, rather than perfection.

We'd rather hear about the failings and struggles of a real person, any day. It makes us feel better about our own problems.

Take your readers on a journey. That's what makes it inspirational! People who are most successful at hawking weight-loss products, for example, aren't the celebs who grew up pin thin – they're the people who started out heavier, and then let people watch them lose the weight. It's all about the journey.

Don't know what you're doing? Great! There's nothing more appealing to readers. 'Here's my passion. Here's my dream. I have *absolutely zero idea what I'm doing* but I invite you to come along with me as I figure it out and make hilarious mistakes along the way.'

Would you read that blog? I would. See, somewhere along the line we've got it all backwards. We think that we have to be perfect, in order for the world to love us. But actually, we just have to be *authentic*, and brave enough to show it. That's what people dig.

## Getting down and dirty

It's all about the *dirt*. There's a famous story about the Beatles. Their producer remastered one of the early recordings and removed all the audio 'dirt', as it's called – all the scratchiness, mistakes, casual conversation in the background. And you know what? No one bought the recording. No one liked it. It was too sterile, antiseptic. It was boring.

> **It's all about the dirt. The dirt gives it flavour, personality, character, style.**

A personal story about dirt: my grandfather was a cowboy. He used to come in from his horseback ride, clank across the tiled floor, still wearing his spurs on his boots, and make a cherry pie with his unwashed, horse-y hands. He'd mix the dough with his hands, throw it up in the air, where it would stick to the ceiling, and then catch it as it came down. (He was a very cool guy, my grandfather.)

Now, as you might imagine, my grandmother absolutely loathed this entire procedure. She'd nag him to 1) Take off his spurs and 2) Wash his dirty hands before he touched the food.

'But,' he'd say, all innocence, 'the dirt is the flavour.'

And sure enough, his cherry pies were always the best that anyone had ever tasted.

## Don't hide your quirks

The dirt is the flavour. Your own peculiar failings, short-comings, eccentricities, quirks. Your hair that frizzes instead of curls.

Your passion for sharpening all the pencils and keeping them in a line. Whatever it is. That's what makes you you. The more detail and accuracy with which you can report your quirky adventures as you take this journey, the more people will love and support your progress.

Listen, when I started this adventure, I had three things:

1. One goat

2. A great view

3. My ability to tell a story.

That was it. No deep pockets, no cash, no business experience. I didn't even know how to milk the damn goat. But I kept diaries about my struggles to learn to live on the farm. I self-published those diaries. I got lucky when the diaries got picked up and republished by Hay House, and Reid Tracey, the CEO of Hay House, got interested in our business and invested in us. And that's how it all started for me.

**You no longer need to wait for anyone to give you permission to tell your own story.**

Social media is one big mouth, waiting for content to feed it. Everyone is consuming content these days, and you can put your content out there for free. You don't even have to have a website – you can do it with a Facebook page and an Instagram account.

BUT. You must tell the truth about your journey.

### *It's not about you – it's about your business*

Does the thought horrify you? Don't think so much about presenting yourself to the world. Instead focus on what you're really passionate about, in your business. Remember, passion is in the details. Concentrate on what really gets you going, about what you're doing, and why it's important to you to share that with the world. You have a responsibility to walk your gift into the world – it can't do it alone. You're going to have to go with it. Imagine it like the first day of school, when your child is going for the first time, at around four years old.

Would you chuck your child out into the parking lot, and say, 'Good luck, kid – door's over there'?

No, of course not! What kind of mother would that make you? You take your child in, introduce them to the teacher, show them around, make sure they're comfortable and happy. It's not about you, on that day – it's about them. You're not too shy to walk them into school because that's your job.

And it's the same with your gift.

**Focus on your passion, and it will
remove your self-consciousness.**

By a happy coincidence, this is also how you develop leadership presence. Anyone doing anything with complete, passionate focus is fun to watch. Have you ever sneakily watched a little kid playing, when they don't know you're watching? Of course you have. Fascinating, isn't it? There's not a lot going on in terms of narrative, maybe – but the complete concentration with which they focus on the task makes it brilliantly entertaining.

Passion is interesting. Focus on your passion, and be brave enough to share your journey. That will be the spine of what you can share with your readers, and help you produce great social media content.

## A picture tells a thousand words

Perfection is the last thing that you want your customers to see. Side note: it's not that image doesn't matter – because it does. If you're taking photographs to push your business and further your brand, of course the images count. You want them to tell a story, and everything matters – the subliminals count. When I'm having photographs taken of the goats (and yes, ma'am, I splurge on a professional photographer, she's worth every penny!) I take those pictures on a sunny day. The pictures of goats free-ranging on the grass, in the sunshine, send a different subliminal message than the pictures of goats on a grey day.

If you're running a Montessori childcare business, you need to take pictures of yourself with children outside, in a forest setting – not in an industrial room! But rather than making yourself crazy trying to make it 'perfect', think about making it aligned. Congruent.

## What is the presence that you want your customers to receive?

Personally, I've got to be honest: I wish we were taking pictures 20 years ago, when I had fewer chins and more collagen. But, hey-ho. I've worked out that what I want my clients to receive when they look at me is reassurance. I'm a mother, and a grandmother. My concern is to develop natural healing remedies that people can use on their own health journey. I want to combat the feeling of helplessness and powerlessness that people get when they go to the doctor and the person in the white coat isn't able to help them. I want my clients to feel empowered to be the expert of their own wellness, and I want to give them the tools for that. So reassurance is where we're at. And a motherly, grandmotherly presence is fine for that – I don't need to be a bikini babe. Which – at this point in my life – is a damn good thing!

So think carefully about what presence you want your customers to receive from you. Chances are, perfection won't even show up on the list. Because let's be honest – we all hate and resent those fake people who present themselves as completely perfect. And hatred and resentment aren't the emotions you want to inspire in your clients!

It's the dirt that makes you who you are. So put your boots on the road, and revel in that cloud of dirt. You're moving!

# Step 7

# TURN OBSTACLES INTO OPPORTUNITIES

Learn to TAT – or 'Try, Assess, Tweak'. Embracing change. The meaning of failure. You're just trying it – and that's okay! Here's how to convert every obstacle into a launch pad. What to do if you fail.

I've promised you that the journey itself will teach you all you need to know along the way – but how, exactly, does that occur?

There's a specific and very simple technology behind it – I call it TAT. It stands for Try, Assess, Tweak. Nothing could be more straightforward.

## Take the plunge and start learning

Starting something new that terrifies you? No problem!

## Task 1: Try

This one might seem obvious, but you'd be amazed at the number of people who just sit on their sofa and never take that first step. I remember when I was writing my very first book. I'd taken a leave of absence from my day job as a journalist. A very risky endeavour, obviously. I was terrified. I was working in a coffee house because my home office was just too still and quiet. And I wish I had a free skinny latte for every person who wandered up to me and asked me what I was doing.

(...Nothing at the moment, because I'm sitting here answering your silly questions!)

And then they'd say – 'You're writing a book? Wow, I've always wanted to write a book! I've got the greatest story. I just wish I had the time!'

(...Hmmm... If you'd sit down at your own table and get to work, we'd both have the time to write!)

You take my point. What were these people waiting for – the time fairy to come by and strike them with her magic wand? Nobody was going to magically grant them the time to write that book.

**No one gives you the time to pursue a heart project and build your business or do whatever it is that you want to do. You find the time. You make the time. You steal the time.**

You claw the time from the margins of your day. But there's all the difference in the world between you and those annoying people in the coffee shop, because you're actually going to try it, and put your boots on the road.

Trying is the first step.

## Task 2: Assess

This simply means that after you try something, you look at it to see how you did. Seems obvious – but again, you'd be amazed at the number of people who blunder around, making the same mistakes time after time. Assessment happens by asking two questions:

1. What worked?

2. What do I need to change, to take it to the next level?

Continually asking these two questions about everything you do will develop your own *best practice*. Best practice is your personal bible – it's the code you live by. You've developed it – it fits you, your business, your locale, your product, your service. It's your very own operating manual.

Treat yourself to a brand new blank book, title it 'BEST PRACTICE' and start capturing all the things that you know work for you. Who knows, someday you might publish it in a book like this one, to help other people along the way! We all have to develop continually and share our own best practice with one another – it's how we'll survive as a species.

**Collecting and writing down best practice
is an invaluable process because it works
against the normal flow of your brain.**

Normally, your brain scans your environment and picks out all the negative, scary things to focus on. It does this to keep you alive; it's a great survival mechanism. But this default isn't always helpful. It's important to train your brain to focus on *what works* instead of what's a problem. Let me give you an example:

### Find out what really works

In 1991, a man named Jerry Sternin was named Director of the charity Save the Children in Vietnam and given what seemed like an insurmountable challenge. More than 65 per cent of all children living in Vietnamese villages were malnourished at the time, and government officials wanted Sternin to create an effective, large-scale programme to combat child malnutrition and to show results within six months – with very little budget.

Impossible, you might think! But Sternin did something very clever: he identified poor families whose children *weren't* malnourished despite the fact that they were facing the same challenges and obstacles as their neighbours and had no access to any special resources.

What were these families doing, that was working?

He discovered that these families collected tiny shrimps, crabs, and fish from paddy fields, and added those – along with sweet potato greens, boiled rice, and what other food was available – to their children's meals. These foods were accessible to everyone, but most community members believed they were inappropriate for young children. The non-starving families were also feeding their children three to four times a day.

Result! The pilot project resulted in the sustained rehabilitation of several hundred malnourished children and the promotion of social change in their communities.

---

If a problem seems insurmountable, find the little bit that's working – and do more of that. Hewlett Packard calls this 'amplifying the positive deviance', which is a boring name. I call it Do What Works.

Assessing everything you do, after you do it, will allow you to build you own personal body of best-practice knowledge. You'll get better, and know more, every day. Your daily experience will be an education – because you'll be learning and improving continuously.

### Task 3: Tweak

Tweaking means that you act on the principles of Best Practice you've distilled, and change what you're doing accordingly. As a heart-led business, you have to be mobile, flexible, adaptive. The Vietnamese families with children who were starving were following tradition; the families whose children were thriving were able to go against convention and adopt a new habit.

**You need to be as alert and responsive as a sailor is to shifts in the wind.**

Did you know that an aeroplane is off course 99 per cent of the time it's in the air? It's true! The pilot's job is continually to bring the plane back on course so that it arrives on schedule at its destination. That's you. That's your job.

Become comfortable with constantly adjusting your flight path, because that's how it works. Not perfection – never perfection. Instead, continual attention, constant assessment and immediate response.

## Embrace change

One of the fierce facts about our lives today is that the pace of change isn't only breathtaking but constantly accelerating. The world of 50 years ago was much faster than the world of 500 years ago, when Copernicus suggested that it just might be the Earth spinning around the Sun instead of the other way around. And change at the beginning of the Renaissance occurred much faster than it did 50,000 years ago, where things remained the same for centuries on end.

These days new developments don't take decades to emerge – they flash by in a year, six months, a month. Until 2004, Amazon was just a bookseller. In the short time since then, the growth of home delivery has completely revolutionized the face of business everywhere and is now busily killing off high-street shops that have been around forever. The Kindle wasn't even invented until 2007, and who could imagine the world without it now?

But some eternal principles remain the same. As it was in the day of the dinosaurs, so it is today: you change, or you die. Nowhere is this more true than in business. In an environment of accelerating change, your ability to adapt and actively embrace change isn't just positive, it's critical.

To succeed, you're going to need to practise succession – the art of allowing one stage to follow another at the perfect time.

## You can't succeed if you're clinging to the past when you should be moving forward.

Don't resist and dismiss change – lean in to it. Read the papers, and think about how the trends you spot there will affect your baby business. Whatever it is, it probably does affect your business because the world is changing, and you need to pay attention to the way it's going.

The same can be said about your business. It's constantly changing. It's changing, you're changing, the situation around you is changing. It's important to be aware of that, and not to get too attached to doing things in a certain way. The goalposts are constantly moving. Nothing is permanent. Everything is in transition.

If you accept this, it's fine. It's only the getting-stuck part that's painful. Imagine that you're in a canoe, being carried rapidly down a river. It's only going to hurt if you reach out and try to hold onto something on the shore.

Unhappy with the way things are going? Great, it's going to change soon. Happy with the way things are going? Too bad, it's going to change soon. Embrace it! Change is the only constant.

## The lost photo opportunity

Here's a little cautionary tale about embracing change. I've always thought that one of the best examples of failing to do this is the Kodak company. In 1974, Kodak held 90 per cent of the world's film market. Think of the term 'a Kodak moment'. Kodak *was* cameras, film, and everything to do with photography. But where are they now? In 2012 Kodak filed for bankruptcy, beaten by their failure to embrace the digital camera. They asked the wrong question: 'How do we sell more film?' instead of asking the right question: 'How do we help our customers tell their stories?'

Here's a twist that makes this story even more ironic. The inventor of the first digital camera, back in 1975, was a guy named Steve Sasson – and he worked for Kodak at the time. That's right: the invention that would take over the photography world was right in front of them. They owned it. And they crushed it and turned away out of fear. For Kodak's leaders, going digital meant killing film, smashing the company's golden egg to make way for the new. They were too afraid – and so they failed to embrace the innovation that would change the world of film.

They turned into dinosaurs that day and became extinct. It just took a further four decades for them to fall over.

---

So where are your 'digital cameras', those developments coming along to threaten the future of what you're currently doing? Where are the ideas that you're ignoring for fear they'll upset the status quo? What are you not embracing in your business that might become the future without you?

Don't just accept change or tolerate change. Embrace change. Chase change. Create change. Find the curve – and get ahead of it.

> **As a new, small, agile and nimble business, the ability to turn on a dime is your strength. Work it.**

For the challenge of coping with the rapid pace of change around us, I like to turn to nature as a teacher. You know who has this nailed? Trees. No matter what occurs in the world around us, trees are still here. They can't run, and they can't hide, but they manage to survive and do their thing, beautifully, millennia after millennia.

So, what can we learn from trees, about dealing with change?

Trees are flexible. They bend with the wind.

Tree have roots which keep them stable.

Trees need other trees. They survive best in the ecosystem of a forest.

This is the basic outline for surviving change triumphantly. Stay flexible on top; deep-rooted to your values; and connected to a flourishing ecosystem. The trees had it sussed the whole time. Be like a tree!

## The flexibility to thrive

When we started out five years ago, it was just me, making soap in my farmhouse kitchen. Then my husband quit his day job and joined me, milking the goats and making kefir. Today there are 25 of us on the team. What I do on a daily basis has changed beyond recognition. These days, I spend my time in the office, managing the team, doing marketing work, writing, communicating with clients and, recently, a lot of press.

Luckily for me, I like all of these things. I knew diddly-squat about how to manage a team when I started – but I've learned through time (and making some horrific mistakes!) and, mostly, it's pretty good fun.

My husband, on the other hand, loathes the management part of it. He hates paperwork and can't stand managing people. So he doesn't come to our daily morning meetings; instead, he oversees the physical side of things, circulates through the factory and the farm during the day, keeping an eye on people, sticking his head into different departments and checking on things. He fixes things that are broken, solves problems, designs equipment and monitors workflow. His function is different to mine – and different to how it used to be.

## We've each found our place in the new system that's grown up around us.

We've hired my brother-in-law Rhys to come and work with us (he's part-time with us, part-time physics teacher at a local school) and the two Jones brothers are generally to be found together, out on the farm somewhere, managing the farm, working with tractors or diggers or Land Rovers, constructing new buildings and repairing infrastructure.

We've also hired our daughter and her husband to come and work with us. Elly runs the office, and Josh is our production manager. They both do a brilliant job. Someday, when our day is done, Elly will take over from me, and Josh will take over from Rich. Everything changes. We're turning responsibilities over to them slowly, one at a time, as seems appropriate.

Five years from now, Elly and Josh will be running more things than they are today – and Rich and I will have stepped back a bit more than we are at the present. Although Rich says that he doubts my ability to retire, and I'm certainly not feeling it at the moment! But no doubt I'll feel differently five years from now. Everything changes.

## Developing new skills

Because of this fact, I've actually fallen in love with statistics. I used to say that I was a words girl, not a numbers person, and I was baffled by anyone who was good at maths.

But I love looking at sales figures now, because they tell me what's happening. Turns out, I can see patterns in the numbers, and it's cool to watch! We launched a baby line. It's not performing particularly well. Why not? No idea. It's a good product, and it should be a natural fit. But boots on the road show me that it's not. So we accept that, we trim it back and leave room for something else to grow. Like pruning a plant, you cut back the dead wood, and prune for growth. Without the sales figures, I don't know where to prune. Watching the stats shows me where the changes are – and where they need to be as we move forward.

**Look for the places where your business is changing and go with it.**

Don't resist change, or pretend it's not happening. Read industry magazines, and get used to the idea of future-proofing. Where do you think your industry is heading? What will it be like in five years, in 10 years? Your guess is as good as anyone's. Imagine your little business growing and developing, five years on from today. Be prepared to shift as the situation alters. Hold the big picture of change and growth, and pay attention.

This is why it's so important to learn how to TAT – because everything is changing, all the time. What worked yesterday might not work tomorrow. But if you continue to TAT as you move forward, you'll always stay adapted to the current environment.

## What if you fail?

As a species, we're very fearful of failure. In the UK in 2017, 35.85 per cent of respondents aged 18-64 reported that fear of failure would stop them from setting up a business. In the USA that number drops to 33.36 per cent. Still, it's more than a third of people who let their fear stop them from moving ahead.

Don't be that cat.

I think of failure slightly differently to most people – which might be why I'm so willing to entertain it. And I do fail – oh, yes, I fail a lot! I'm the girl who failed more than anyone else. I just got up and dusted myself off more. I have an empowering belief about failure. To my mind, failure is simply a measure of risk.

It's like a counter. You can move it in one direction or another. If you never fail, it means you're never taking any risks. No good!

On the other hand, if you fail all the time, it's probably because you're taking too many risks.

I like to set my success–failure ratio counter at about 80–20, which is a magic proportion for a lot of things. If I succeed 80 per cent of the time, and fail 20 per cent of the time, I figure that I'm taking about the right number of risks. If I'm failing 50 per cent of the time – I'm taking too many risks. Time to dial it back a bit.

> **If I'm never failing at all, then I know that I need to paddle out into the deeper waves, stand up on the surfboard and let the ocean slap me around! No risk, no gain.**

So I look for a 20 per cent failure rate. That's how I know I'm taking enough chances. I look for 20 per cent failure in myself, and in my team. I tell them that, when they join. And when they fail – hurray! Write it down in the journal and add it to your 20 per cent.

And then Assess it. And then Tweak it.

And then Try it again.

## *Step* 8

# HOW TO MOTIVATE YOURSELF

The secret tech tool that will allow you to accomplish almost anything. And guess what – you probably already own one! Create your own structure. Be immaculate. Rock your uniform. Hit your marks.

The task facing you at the moment may seem mountainous, overwhelming, insurmountable. Where to begin? There are so many things that need to be done, all of them important. And working as hard as I'm sure you already are, is draining, so the time left over for anything is probably minimal. Much less for changing the world!

So here's a happy little secret that you can tuck in your back pocket – *everything*, no matter how mahoosive, can be broken down into smaller chunks. I call this – not-so-originally – *chunking*.

*'Inspiration exists, but it has to find you working.'*

Pablo Picasso

## Overcoming the sensation of feeling overwhelmed

Overwhelm is the enemy. It's simply too tempting, when faced with something huge – a giant task like starting a business or a massive problem like plastic in the oceans – to stand on the sand and bleed out into the ocean, and just die of despair. It's too big, it's too much; what can one person possibly do?

Eco-anxiety is a thing. Research shows that 34 per cent of British people experience some level of eco-anxiety; among 16- to 24-year-olds, 40 per cent feel overwhelmed by the crisis.

We can't spare any eco-warriors. We can't afford for anyone to be hamstrung by anxiety. We need everyone who cares to be geared up and fighting. So no, you're not allowed to give in to despair and overwhelm, and bleed out into the ocean. Over anything.

*Overwhelm is the enemy.* Say it over and over to yourself. Say it while you're staring in the mirror.

### Fixing the ocean, one rock pool at a time

And here's my answer to overwhelm – the alternative to bleeding out into the ocean over all the things that need to be done. I call it 'Rock Pool Technology'.

Fixing the ocean is too big. But – how about fixing up one tiny rock pool, or yard of beach? That much we can each handle. Pick out one rock pool and make it your own. Clean it up. Make it beautiful, stock it with creatures and watch over them fiercely. If everyone on earth did that, the ocean would be fixed.

Your rock pool needs to become your focus. Dig a small hole, and dig it deep. Don't try to make your business be everything to everyone – you'll be spreading yourself too thin.

## If you pick one thing and do it exquisitely well, you'll gain the trust of your customers.

Later on, they'll trust you to do other things as well. But that day isn't today. Today, you're focusing on your rock pool only.

This laser focus becomes a practice that protects you from overwhelm. You can turn it on anything. And here's how the technology works:

### 1. Break it down.

Whatever it is, it can be chunked into smaller pieces. This is what your journal is for. Just do a big bluuurgh brain dump onto your journal, purging out everything that needs to be done, in no particular order. Emotional outbursts and crayon scribbles welcome at this point. I even do the odd doodle. With big red crayon, if I'm having a 'mean reds' day.

### 2. Prioritize.

Now go back through that brain dump and put things in order of urgency. It may all seem of equal importance when everything is unexamined and still hiding in the nightmare closet of your mind. But once you actually chase it all out into the sunshine and examine it in your journal, everything is *not* equally urgent. Some things need to be done immediately, and some things can wait. Some things can't be done until other things are done first. This bit is best done on the computer because you can type things in, and move them around. So take your journal list, and type it into your computer, as if you're your own secretary. Keep working and reworking it, until you feel that your running list is in order. I like an app called Evernote for this. It's free, and allows you to create lists, notes and notebooks across all your gadgets. You can also save emails, web pages, etc., and organize them into your notebooks. I wouldn't be without it!

### 3. Date-mark all the items on your list.

A to-do list is just a to-do list. But once it has a date, it's a plan. Evernote has a pre-prepared template for notes called 'The Project' that's just my favourite thing *ever*. It gives you a place to enter your Project Title, Time Frame (start date and deadline), Brainstorming, Details (purpose, intention, desired outcome), List of Next Actions, Resources (reference notes and delegated items) and general notes. Seriously. It practically does the whole project for you. And here's the beauty of running yourself through that exquisitely organized template – it will train your brain to operate that way. Next time you think of a project, you'll rush to your Evernote project template. You'll refine your purpose and intention, set yourself a time frame, break down your intention into next actions, find resources and think of things you can delegate. It sets you up for success, right there. So go forth and download!

### *The secret motivation device you probably already own*

Before you begin, though, you need one more tool. And the good news on this one is that you probably already own one!

Here's the story behind this magic instrument: when I was a university student, I had the great privilege of taking a long-narrative writing course with the brilliant author Isabel Allende. She told us that the difference between writing a poem and writing a long-narrative form like a book is simply the discipline of working every day. When you're writing a poem, you can wait for inspiration to strike. When you're writing a book, you have to show up day after day.

And she suggested to us the same tool that I'm going to suggest to you now: *a common kitchen timer*. That's right, this simple piece of equipment is the true Holy Grail of motivation. Who knew?

Here's how it works. Have a project that you want to begin? Great. Set your kitchen timer for 60 minutes and promise yourself that you'll stop when the 60 minutes is up. Begin. Work for an hour. When the timer goes off, you stop.

Simple! And yet – world-changing. Here's why:

> ### You can do anything for 60 minutes. It makes the task do-able. Repeat that exercise every day, and you'll move mountains.

Want to write a book, but feel overwhelmed by the task? Here's the secret: you never have to write an entire book. You only have to sit down for 60 minutes at a time. Over time, those 60-minute sessions add up to a book! I've done five of them like that. Works a treat.

### Look back at how far you've come

Chunk it, break it down, prioritize it, put a deadline on each item and then sit down with your kitchen timer to work through those chunks, 60 minutes at a time. Look back in a few short weeks, and you'll be astonished at how far you've come, and how much you've achieved. Join us on the WATT Facebook page, and we'll applaud you when you complete each chunk – that's what community is for!

## Refilling the well

Self-care is, ironically, the first thing that gets tossed out of the window when an already busy person with many responsibilities starts his or her own business. But it shouldn't be.

Because... no one can drink from an empty well. You're the well. People come to drink from you every day. Parents, children, animals, partners – and once you start your business, you'll add clients, suppliers and team members to that list. You're the source of water, and everyone's going to turn up with their teacup, wanting a swig.

But what happens when the well runs dry?

**What happens when you finally give away the last drop of energy, resource, inspiration that you have – and there's no more left?**

Everyone is going to go thirsty. So, you can't afford to let that happen. I know: you probably don't care so much about

114

yourself. But you *do* care about everyone you love. Think about what will happen to them if you let the well run dry.

How do you avoid that? You refill the well. And you take it as an ongoing practice, before the well runs dry. Don't let it get that far.

### The magic touch

When you nurture yourself, you tap into the mammalian care-giving system. Turns out, you don't have to be cared for by someone else. You can DIY this one! One important way the care-giving system works is by triggering the release of oxytocin. Research indicates that increased levels of oxytocin strongly increase feelings of trust, calm, safety, generosity, and connectedness, and facilitate the ability to feel warmth and compassion for ourselves.

Oxytocin is released inside your system during breastfeeding, orgasm, when parents interact with young children, or when human beings caress one another. A good long hug will do! Because thoughts and emotions have the same effect on our bodies, whether they're directed to ourselves or to others, this research suggests that self-compassion may be a powerful trigger for the release of oxytocin.

## So by looking after yourself, you're hacking your own biology.

You can literally calm and comfort yourself with soothing touch. You might feel a bit strange – but hey, your body doesn't care! It just responds to the physical gesture of warmth and care, just as a baby responds to being held in its mother's arms. Physical touch releases oxytocin, reduces cortisol and calms cardiovascular stress. So next time you're feeling upset, try giving yourself a hug, or stroking or massaging your face or arm, or gently rocking your body. Make a clear gesture that conveys feelings of love, care, and tenderness. If other people are around – be subtle! Give yourself a discreet squeeze by wrapping your arms around yourself. Notice if you feel warmer, softer or calmer after this process. It's amazing how easy it is to tap into the mammalian caregiving system and change your bio-chemical experience.

## Ask yourself: What do I do to get my mojo back?

Refilling the well is a practice of self-care and self-nurturance. What do you do right now, to refill the well? What are the things that you do purely for yourself, to bring back your mojo and get you back on track, refreshed, reinvigorated and re-inspired?

It's funny, when I first ask this question to women who have recently joined the WATT group, they tend to look at me blankly. 'I… take a bath?' they say doubtfully. 'Go for a walk?'

You need to get good at filling the well. You need to become an expert. In fact, you need to be taking care of yourself with the same degree of care and nurturance that you turn on everyone around you.

**What would that look like – if you took care of yourself with the same degree of loving kindness that you devote to your loved ones?**

What would it feel like? You have no idea, do you? Because most of us never even consider it. We're the last people on the list – the last to get food, the last to demand a day off, the last to do what we want to do.

You need to reverse that thinking, right now. Because if you burn out and fall over, then everyone who depends on you will fall over too.

I'd like you to open your journal, right now, and write, 'Ten ways to refill the well'. Ten activities that you can do, whenever you need to, that make you feel happy and juicy and fulfilled.

You're your own boss now. You're responsible for your own self-care, nurturance and inspiration – because you're going to have to inspire the people around you. You're going to release your own oxytocin!

## Your health is your wealth

While we're on the subject of looking after yourself, I'd like to suggest that you develop some health-promoting habits. If you're ill and exhausted, you're not going to have enough energy to run your own business. Here are some very straightforward, simple hacks you can employ to boost your energy and feel your best so you can drive your business to success.

### *Take a good multi-strain probiotic every day*

Whether it's my kefir or someone else's probiotic, I don't care. I'm not trying to sell anything to you here. Just take it. Take it every day. We now know that your gut microbiome is so important to your health that it's considered to be an additional organ in your body. Your gut microbiome determines how much energy you have, how well you sleep, how much pain you're in, and how much anxiety/depression you're experiencing. It's no use putting all these great new habits to work if you're biochemically incapable of functioning well and feeling good because your gut microbiome is damaged. Every day, your microbiome is being assaulted by antibiotics in the food chain and ground water, stress, pollution, sugar and environmental toxins. Those things are killing off important strains of bacteria in your gut, just like pouring bleach into a river kills the fish. You must push back against that process daily with a good-quality, multi-strain probiotic. Just make sure that it's pure, unflavoured and free of any sweeteners, sugar or chemicals.

## Take a complete prebiotic every day

The kefir – or other multi-strained probiotic of your choice – puts the fish into the river of your gut. But then you have to feed those fish. Gut bugs eat fibre. This means that you need a high-fibre diet, in order to feed your gut bugs. But what kind of fibre, exactly, do you need? Some of your gut bugs eat exotic fibres that can only be found in exotic items like cassava flour, which is a bit hard to come by in the local supermarket. So we need a complete prebiotic that supplies the harder-to-find fibres that our gut bugs need.

## Eat an anti-inflammatory diet

Get rid of the high-GI bread, potatoes, pasta, rice. Cut way back on sugar, cow dairy, gluten. Instead, eat lots of vegetables, fruits, good fats, like olive oil and oily fish, and 'good grains' that are gluten-free and low-GI, like amaranth, millet, oatmeal, quinoa and buckwheat. For more details and information on the anti-inflammatory diet, see my book, *The Kefir Solution: Natural Healing for IBS, Depression and Anxiety.*

## Take a microbiome test

Again, use mine or take someone else's. But get your hands on this information ASAP. This amazing technology has just recently become available, and it truly is life-changing. A microbiome test will show you which bacterial strains you're missing in your own gut system – and tell you exactly what foods you personally need to focus on, to build up the diversity inside your gut. You really can eat your way healthy. Get some answers!

## Be that cat

This is a conversation about duty, and discipline, and responsibility. And doing the right thing. All the time. Let me put it to you this way: imagine two people…

Person A is dutiful. She's responsible. She's *good*. She always gets the house clean, the chores done, a nutritious dinner on the table. She irons. She even irons the pants. She puts names on all the name tapes and sews them onto clothes. She's a pillar of the PTA and she does good works on the weekends. She doesn't have a room for her own projects in her house because she's given the existing space away to everyone else (since they need it more than she does). She gets her Christmas shopping done by the end of November and sends

Christmas cards before December 15. She always puts herself last. She's generally exhausted.

Now consider person B. She's imaginative, creative, wilful. She surprises her family sometimes by serving naughty takeaways. You can't always predict what she's going to say. She's demanding sometimes. She says 'no' sometimes, just because she wants to have a lie-in on a Saturday – and she insists that someone make her a cup of tea and bring it to her in bed. She disappears sometimes, and when questioned, her family will find that she's gone for a walk on her own, or off to find a sacred well, or view an art exhibition. She has hobbies. She pursues her passions. She demands space for her own interests, and her own pursuits. She takes her kids along on butterfly-hunting expeditions.

Now think for a minute. If you were a partner, with whom would you rather be? If you were a child, who would you rather have for a mum?

It's a funny thing – we think that we need to be dutiful, responsible, perfect. And of course, to a certain extent, we do. Ideally, we hit our marks, keep our marriage vows, and show up on time for the school run. *But...*

### Gratitude for a drawer that's full of clean socks never kept a partner from straying.

How many women have exhausted themselves trying to be dutiful and perfect, only to have their lover – and, later, children – dismiss them because they've become boring and dull – in the service of that very same lover and children?

It's passion that keeps you interesting, vivid, alive and vibrant. Your own passions. And if you're a little unpredictable as a result? Great! People love that. It's attractive. It's interesting.

Be that cat. You know that cat who always has their own things going on? Who sometimes is incredibly loving, and sometimes wants to stalk off on their own, tail twitching, doing their own thing? Who ever said, 'Damn, I wish that cat was more boring!' No, everyone's fascinated by that cat. Everyone wants more of that cat. Be *that* cat.

Here's a little hack to help you become more Cat B…

## Become your own producer

When I worked as a radio talk-show host, I was lucky enough to have a 'producer'. Each person who was considered 'talent' had one of these producers assigned to us, and their general mission was to accompany us through our professional day and make our lives work. It was great.

My producer, Beth, would sit with me beforehand and help me brainstorm what I was going to talk about on the show. She'd also check on me during the show when I couldn't leave the radio studio: 'Are you okay?' 'Do you need some water?' 'Do you want some more coffee?' Then she'd screen the calls that came in during the show and stack them in order of preference so that I'd know to whom I should speak first. Beth's role was invisible to the listeners but absolutely indispensable to the production of my radio show.

Her significance was reflected in her job title: she wasn't just an assistant – far from it. She was a partner, a team member, the other half of our duo. As it happened, she was brilliant and funny and became a lifeline in the middle of the night, when I was talking to a million invisible listeners, because things can get weird.

## Life in the real world

As you might imagine, after 10 years of living like this, the real world blew pretty cold and lonely when I no longer had a radio job and – almost more importantly – no longer had a producer. Who would baby me, who would be concerned for me if my voice got rough, who would make me a hot cup of tea, who would phone the people I needed to talk to, and organize our conversations, and print out the things I needed to know, before I needed to know them, and put them on my desk in a tidy stack? Who would schedule my time, bring me the newspapers, so that I could give all my concentration to being creative in the moment?

The answer – it turned out – was me, myself. I became my own producer, and you can too.

Here's how it came about: I had to go somewhere complicated. There were train tickets, hotel, work information, etc., to take care of. This was just the sort of thing that Beth used to organize for me – she'd hand me a 'Go Sheet' with all the details of everything I needed to know, in the order I needed to know it. What time the train departed, where the transfer stops were, the address and phone number of the hotel so that I wouldn't panic at the other end when I arrived.

She wasn't there to do it, so I made my own Go Sheet. It doesn't sound like a big deal, but it made all the difference.

I sat down and organized the trip, printing out everything in a neat folder, as if I was preparing it for someone else. And then I became that someone else and enjoyed the fruits of my labour.

I became my own producer.

## Start considering yourself as 'the talent'. You're the star of your own show.

You're a worthy, worthwhile, creative genius whose gifts need to be given to the world. You're someone who deserves to be looked after, to the very highest standard!

Then switch hats and pretend that you're your own producer. Think about your day tomorrow. If your job was to support 'the talent' with that same schedule, how would you support her? Think through her day. What is she going to wear? Lay it all out, so that she doesn't have to panic in the morning looking for a clean shirt. Something missing a button? Great, it's still the night before and you have time to sew it on for her. Because that's what producers do.

What will she need to get out the door? Lay out her 'launching pad' so that it's all ready in the morning. Purse, keys, bottle of water, papers for the meeting nicely organized in a tidy case. Don't have a carrying case appropriate for whatever line of business you're in? Add it to the list of things to buy for her. You've got to look after the talent. She's the star!

## Own the room

*Everything matters.* If you carry your papers in an appropriate, handsome bag, you feel a million bucks when you enter the room for the meeting. You'll walk in and own that space in an entirely different way than if you're apologizing and scrabbling your papers out of some scabby backpack because you can't afford a proper briefcase 'yet'. Your producer wouldn't *ever* let you walk into a meeting without the right briefcase.

There's a beautiful magic that happens when you lay out your clothes, prepare your launching pad and organize your 'Go Sheet' the night before. When you wake up, it feels like someone else has done it for you, and it's *amazing*. Try it!

You'll nearly weep with gratitude, at the care and attention that *someone* has paid to you. And this person knows all your sizes, and everything! Your morning will be so much easier, and you'll float rather than scramble. Just as talent should.

It protects your nervous system from the screaming and angst that happens when you're racing around looking for your keys because you're about to be late. That kind of thing is violence to your nervous system. It's damaging, and it shouldn't be allowed. A good producer would never allow you to get into that state, because you won't be able to perform properly.

So become your own producer. Because baby, you're worth it!

## Be your own hero

Another reason that it's important to motivate yourself is that you're often the only person around to get the job done. There's no point waiting for Prince or Princess Charming to come and break you out of your current life or situation. Because I've got news for you – despite the fairy tales that promise us rescue, no one is coming.

How do I know? It's another story from my time at the radio station when I worked with Beth. I was 26 years old, and KGO Radio was the largest station in the San Francisco Bay Area. At night, the 50,000-watt signal ran all the way from Canada to Mexico, pulling in more than a million listeners.

My show was on from 10 p.m. to 1 a.m., five days a week. Beth and I were two young women of the same age, in a world of male talk-show hosts.

## It felt like just the two of us against the world.

We were a tight team, especially at that time of night, when everyone else in the radio station had gone home.

My job was to scan five newspapers every day and pick out the most controversial topics to fuel my news talk show. I quickly learned that making lots of people angry was the safest and most efficient way to make sure that all 11 phones lines were lit up. There's nothing worse, trust me, than trying to run a radio talk-show with no callers! It's a nightmare. So I quickly became an expert on infuriating large numbers of people, all at the same time.

One unfortunate side effect of this was that by baiting the National Rifle Association, the Republicans, the racists and the far right, I attracted a large number of political enemies. We received more than our fair share of hate mail and bomb threats. We talked to the police, and they gave us a little seminar on how to identify credible threats. Turns out a credible threat is:

1. repeated

2. tied to a specific time

3. threatening a specific action

They also advised us to take a different route home every night so that we wouldn't be easily followed.

One night, we got a credible bomb threat. 'If you stay on the air, we will bomb the radio station at midnight,' the scrawled message read. It came in over the fax machine three times, over the course of several hours before the show started.

It ticked all the boxes: repeated, specific time, specific action. Beth and I dithered about what to do. We called our bosses – no one picked up. We left messages – no return calls. At around 11 p.m. we called the police. They came in, searched the radio station, and left – just before midnight, we noted.

At five minutes before midnight, Beth and I stared at each other. What to do? Should we shut the entire 50,000-watt radio station down, and leave the building? Leave all the paid advertisements un-aired? It had never happened before, not in the history of the station. If we did it, and the threat wasn't real, we'd be fired from our jobs.

### But if the threat was real, we'd be blown sky high. Is any job worth that?

Beth looked at me through the glass wall that separated us.

'No one's coming, are they?' she said.

'What do you mean?' I asked.

'Well, in all the stories, someone comes to rescue you. A prince on a white horse. A policeman. The army. The boss. But we've called everyone – and no one's coming. It's just us.'

'You're right,' I agreed. 'It's just us.'

### It's all down to you

We took the decision to stay on the air. We both called home and left messages on our own phone machines for our families, just in case. The clock ticked over to midnight – and nothing happened. No bomb. No explosion. We each took a deep breath of relief and went on with the show.

But I've never forgotten the lesson I learned that night.

> **No one is coming. No one is coming to tell you to give your life meaning and purpose.**

No one is coming to release you from that dead-end job. No one is coming to give you the time off to write that book. No one is coming. It's just you.

Even if you're lucky enough to find a supportive partner – and for me, that process took four long decades to achieve! – things happen to people. They die. They change. They get ill. They leave. At the end of the day, your personal adventure is your own responsibility and no one else's. There's no one to blame – and there's no one to organize your rescue. It's just you.

So, what are you going to do about it?

Rescue yourself. You can be your own hero.

## On-the-job branding

At Chuckling Goat, we have a uniform. We call it 'kit'. It's a navy-blue top – polo, T-shirt or rugby shirt, depending on the season – with our logo on it. You can wear whatever you want on the bottom half as long as it's dark in colour, appropriate and non-obtrusive. We also have fleeces, outdoor jackets and bobble hats for winter. These days, when you walk into the team meeting, it's a sea of navy blue!

I started having a uniform back in the day when it was just myself and one assistant. We had one polo shirt each. I bought these shirts with some of the earliest profits I made from selling those first bars of soap.

These days our dairy workers have crisp white coats, as do our nutritionists. When team members are labelling bottles, they wear long green coats, and when they're making soap, they wear long blue coats. Milkers wear special Chuckling Goat overalls. You might think we're a small company to take all this trouble and expense over what people wear. I'll just say it again – everything matters.

> It changes the way people look, the way
> they feel, the way they hold themselves,
> the pride they take in their work.

128

## Rock your uniform

I love having a uniform. I think it makes a huge difference. And I'd encourage you to create a uniform right away, as soon as you've settled on your business name, logo and colour. Getting your logo embroidered onto a T-shirt, polo shirt or fleece is dead cheap, and very worthwhile.

Here's why:

### *It makes you feel and look professional*

Everything matters. You're constantly picking up subliminal cues from what's happening all around you. You're also sending these cues to other people and to yourself. If you slop down to the breakfast table in your bunny slippers and gown and start the day that way because, after all, you're working at home and no one can see you – you'll be sending the following cues to your own brain:

- 'This doesn't really matter'

- 'I don't really care'

- 'I might as well go back to bed'

That's anti-motivation, all the way! When you're working on your business, you're a professional. You're your own boss – and you work for a demanding manager, who has the highest possible standards. Get up, take a shower, pull your hair back neatly, put on your uniform. You're at work, dammit!

## It sends a professional message to people around you

If those people are your family, it makes them realize that you're serious, and that they need to take you seriously. If you wear your uniform when you're out and about, people may even ask you questions about it and you may drum up business. In the early days, we had the phrase 'Why did the goat chuckle?' written on the back on our work shirts. It was a great conversation starter! (Answer by the way: Because she was only kidding. Don't look at me – it was my husband's idea.)

## It draws a line between home and work

One of the most difficult things about working from home is that everything gets blurred together – you're always working, or kind-of working, and never really off-duty. You need to set hours for yourself, and a uniform helps. Assign yourself fixed working hours on your calendar, and stick to them. Wear your uniform when you're working, and take it off when you're finished, and go and spend time with your family. It might not seem like much, but this little exercise makes a huge difference! Keep the edges of your schedule – and your uniform – crisp.

## It creates team solidarity

When a newbie joins the team these days, I'm always amazed at how much they stand out, in their 'own clothes'. The first thing we do is get their size and order them kit. On the first day that they wear their new kit to work, looking like a part of the team and fitting in with everyone else, they immediately look so much more relaxed and happy! Everyone likes to fit in, belong and be part of something larger than themselves. Uniforms create that part-of-the-team feeling.

## Hit your marks

If you're working from home, things can easily get too relaxed. One way to deal with this is to sharpen what you're doing, like putting hospital corners on a bed. Make an agreement with yourself that you'll be immaculate with your timekeeping. Run the clock, rather than letting the clock run you.

I call this 'radio time', from my days on the radio. When I was on the air and it was time for the news at the top of the hour, that broadcast hit at 00:00:00. Not five seconds, or two minutes later – but right on the hour. That's radio time! It's exact.

Everything matters. When we start our morning meetings, we start at 8 a.m. exactly – radio time. Not two minutes past, or five minutes past. Employees who come in late are asked to sharpen their time management. They never do it twice. And when I walk into the room at exactly eight o'clock, dressed in my kit and ready to run the meeting – everyone is there ready, seated in a circle, also wearing kit and waiting for me.

We're a family business, and we work on a farm, overlooking the sea. The office is open-plan, and our management style is very informal and friendly. Even more reason to keep those edges crisp – so that everything doesn't blur into a squashy mass of too much sloppy informality.

This is structure. Everyone needs structure. You need structure.

> When you work for yourself, you have
> to create your own structure. No one
> is going to create it for you.

Introducing a uniform is one way to create structure. Hitting your time marks is another. When you set yourself working hours on your calendar, respect them. When your timer goes off, respect it. Set a mark, and meet it. Your agreements with yourself, and with everyone else, need to be immaculate.

## Create a sense of professional pride

If you say you're going to do something, do it. If you say you're going to deliver something, deliver it. If you tell your kid that you're going to finish work at 4 p.m. and go outside to kick the football, do it. Don't finish at five minutes past four, or ten past. Do it right on the dot – because your commitment to your child is every bit as important as your commitment to a supplier, or a customer. It's a fractal, remember – the pattern is the same, all the way up and down. Being immaculate about making and keeping agreements is the way you create and instil professional pride in yourself and your team.

'Professional' is the biggest compliment that I can give anyone. To me, that means that they hit their marks. They deliver what they promise. They show up on time, neat and tidy. They perform. They make it happen.

Whether or not anyone is watching you – be professional.

# *Step* 9

# HOW TO DEAL WITH
# EVERYONE ELSE

---

**How to get what you want. Do you have
I-itis? Flipping the I–You ratio. How to have
a difficult conversation. Raising the bar.**

---

Okay, so you've motivated yourself – you're chunking, you've got your kitchen timer going, you're rocking your uniform, working as your own producer and hitting your marks. You are, in fact, Cat B.

But how about the rest of the world? How do you change other people's behaviour?

Imagine that your customer is in front of you, and you want to move them from point A to point B. Unless you have enough money to bribe them, power to threaten them, or are prepared to be violent enough to force them – there's only one way to get people to do something.

You have to offer them something that they want.

This means two things:

1.  You have to offer them real, legitimate value. This can't be a scam.

2.  You need to figure out what their needs are and help them meet those needs.

When you think about it, this should be really obvious – but they certainly don't teach it in school!

## Walk a mile in their shoes

To figure out what people want, you're going to need to think about them. Who are they? What drives them? What are they afraid of? What are their pain points? What big problem could you help them solve? You're only going to get what you want by helping them get what they want.

**Astonishingly, when most people write copy for their business website or Facebook page, they spend most of their time speaking about themselves.**

They ask these questions: 'What do I want to say?' 'How do I want to present myself?' 'How can I best describe my business?'

If you've got more 'I' than 'You' in there, you've got a problem I call 'I-itis'.

Do a quick review of your website copy, then have a look through your emails. What's your I–You ratio? That is, how many times do you see the word 'I' as opposed to the word 'You'? Don't worry – it's a very common disorder! And easily fixed.

Your I–You ratio should always favour the word 'you'. Start as many sentences as possible with the word 'you'. After all, it's your customers' favourite word. Start with 'you' and you're automatically addressing their number one topic of interest.

You simply need to put the focus on your customer. It's not about what you want to say – it's about what they need to hear, in order for them to make a decision.

An easy way to start is to begin your sentence with the word 'you'. This forces your brain into a new pattern. It's a practice, to become customer-centric. You'll find your brain rebelling against it at first – and then it will become habit, and you'll wonder how you ever did anything else.

## Who's your perfect customer?

Your business exists to bring value to your customer. End of. Find a need, fill a need.

Start by writing a story about your perfect customer. Who is she? (Or he?) Give her a name. How old is she? Where does she live? Does she have a family, partner, pets? Once you've got her profile clear in your mind, dig deeper. What does she eat? Drink? What frightens her? What are her daily problems? How is her health? What kind of car does she drive? What will happen to her in five years?

> Once you've got a really strong sense of
> her, you're ready to start figuring out how
> you can offer her what she needs.

Flipping your I–You ratio is one of the fastest, most efficient ways to revolutionize your marketing copy – and make it easier to write as well! In the course of changing your copy, you'll also change your mindset – and fix your focus firmly on your customers' needs. Always and forever.

## Figure out the other person's real agenda

Everyone has their own agenda. People want different things. Some people want money. Some want love. Some want family connection. Some want to be number one, or contribute, or learn. People have different value drivers.

Remember when we went through your best possible day in your imagination, and distilled from that your own value drivers? Well, now you need to start doing that for your customers – and for the people around you. You want what you want – but they may want something different. Think about your partner, or your closest friend, for example. What do they want? What drives him or her? Spend some time quietly observing this person, who is so close to you. You might think you already know all about them. But have you overlooked things? Have you made assumptions? Have you assumed, for example, that they always want the same things that you do, for the same reasons?

Because that's a dangerous assumption to make. Everyone wants something different. People have their own agendas. Assuming that a loved one wants the same things as you do can lead to large-scale destruction and damage.

## You need to become a student of other people's value drivers. Observe the clues that they give you.

If an employee is driven by family connection, it's no good just offering them a raise and asking them to work longer hours. They're going to be more motivated by a flexible working schedule. Approach the people around you with sacred curiosity, as if you've never seen them before. What do they want? What's driving them?

And then – figure out *how you can help them get it*. That really is the secret to getting what you want. There's someone standing in front of you with an agenda of their own. Do they care what you want? Not really. Not unless they're your partner, sworn to love and cherish you. And even then – sorry, but chances are that they still have their own agenda going on. No matter how much they love you, very few people are entirely selfless.

This isn't manipulative or self-seeking, by the way. It's simply realistic. Most of us are too blinkered and wrapped up in our own movies to understand that everyone else also has their own agenda going on, and that the vast majority of people don't give a monkey's patoot what you want. They care about what *they* want. So you need to be the one with more resources, the one who breaks the chain, who reaches out and begins to care about what they want. Figure it out, and give it to them. In the course of that happening, they'll help you get what you want, as well. That's good business.

## When people fall short of your standards

It won't be long after you start your business that someone will let you down. A material will be inferior; a delivery will be late; someone will fail to hit their mark. Trust me on this. How annoying – especially as you're being immaculate about hitting all of your marks so beautifully!

In the WATT group, I hear a lot of women entrepreneurs agonizing about this. What should they do when a supplier lets them down? Should they say anything? What exactly should they say? What do you do when things go wrong?

> ### Here's the thing to remember:
> ### clear feedback is a gift.

Whoever this supplier is, they absolutely need to know that they have to raise their game. Otherwise, they'll never improve what they're doing. And as you now understand (I hope!) all business is a boots-on-the-road process. You're improving as you move along – and so should they be. We all need to help one another down that road. And offering clear feedback when things go wrong is how you can help someone else along their journey.

We have this idea that conflict destroys relationships – and so we keep our mouths shut, keep a stiff upper lip, and suffer poor service, cold food, products that aren't as described. And no one improves. Things just stay stuck.

Now, I'm not suggesting that you become that nasty diva who complains about everything and makes everyone's life an embarrassing hell. I don't like that woman either.

## Conflict can strengthen bonds

But there's another way to think about this. Consider this possibility: conflict that's intelligently handled can strengthen the bond between two people – or two businesses. Conflict doesn't have to destroy the bond.

It's difficult to get clear feedback in the world. Generally, people just give you a generalized thumbs-up or a thumbs-down without much helpful detail. Loving family members will be unrealistically supportive; jealous strangers will be unreasonably critical. Neither angle is constructive. Learning exactly how to improve your offering is tough. And if someone if willing to give you detailed, helpful feedback, then that's a good thing. A gift.

And if you're willing to give detailed feedback to someone else, about both what's working, and what you need more of, or less of, for them to take their product or service to the next level – that's a gift you're offering them.

First of all, you need to jettison the belief that you shouldn't speak up, or that you're not entitled to have things the way they were agreed, or in the condition for which you paid. Remember, you're Cat B, and Cat B would never put up with mediocre service or undercooked food. Cat B does wonderful work for wonderful pay – and expects to receive the same.

### Raise your standards and your expectation of the world around you.

So something has gone awry. You ask the question: 'How is this an opportunity?' Perhaps in this instance the snarl-up provides an opportunity to strengthen the bond with this supplier. It's given you a chance to chat and connect with this supplier in a professional context.

How do you connect with people? Is it just by saying 'nice' things to them? No ma'am, it's not. It's by demonstrating awareness of their needs. You can be honest and enter the conversation with the clear intention of strengthening the bond. You can demonstrate awareness of their needs *and...* insist that they also become aware of your needs.

That's the bit that's so often missing. We think that we don't have needs. Or that it's okay for people to overlook our needs – or ignore them – or just not care about them. 'Never mind, darling. Mummy will be fine over here in the corner.'

That's not okay. As a business owner (or just as a human being, for that matter!) you have needs. You have a right to have needs. You have a right for those needs to be met.

## How to handle a situation after you've been let down

When a difficult conversation with a supplier is called for, it can be daunting if you don't know where to begin. Here's a formula of words to help you, starting with...

### 1. 'I'm sure you're not aware of this, but here's what's happening at my end.'

This is an important way to enter the conversation because it's laced with empowering and generous beliefs that will grease the wheels of the interaction. This statement clearly carries the implication that:

- You believe that you're speaking to a basically decent person, someone who's trying to do the right thing.

- You believe that they're not aware they're causing a problem.

- You believe that once they become aware of the problem, they're going to be eager to address and fix the problem.

We certainly *hope* this is true! And believing the best of someone from the beginning, is the best way to inspire them to behave that way. Okay, the person might actually be a nasty jerk or be completely incompetent. But if that's the case, you still haven't lost anything by starting off with a generous belief. You can always get narky later on.

It's also incredibly important to avoid making negative assumptions. We often get furious in advance of a difficult conversation, working ourselves into a rage so that our anger will make us feel strong enough for confrontation. But often, the person on the other end of the phone doesn't actually know what our experience is. Chances are, it's not their fault. Maybe we don't even have the whole story right or understand everything that's involved! So enter the conversation with some positive beliefs. It may not end up being the truth – but it won't hurt to start out optimistic!

## 2. 'Here's the issue.'

This is the part where you explain, clearly and simply, what the problem is. Pretty self-explanatory. Avoid assuming that they know what the problem is. They might, or they might not. They certainly don't understand it from your point of view because, as previously discussed, they have their own agenda going.

### 3. 'I wonder if it would be possible to...' or 'I wonder if next time, it would be possible to...?'

And this is the part where you move into problem-solving mode. This time it's done. It's happened. Either they can fix it now, or they can't. If they can't, there's no point in just fuming or screaming at them. The more productive path is to use this as an opportunity to make sure it doesn't happen next time. What have you both learned? How can this be TAT'ed, for both parties? In your ongoing Assessment process, what do you know now that you didn't know before? What do they know now that they didn't know before? What can you Tweak? What can they Tweak? How does this improve your Best Practice, moving forward? How does it improve their Best Practice?

And this is how interaction can strengthen the bond, instead of damaging it. If you make it clear that what you're interested in is improving best practice on both sides – well, you're offering value. The person on the other side of the transaction can understand that. Can appreciate that. Might even – if they're smart – be improved by that. You're offering value, by the way that you're interacting in the world. Your very presence makes things better around you.

I use this principle, every day. People get it wrong. It happens. Our suppliers – our couriers – make mistakes. When this happens, I pick up the phone. (Much better than email for this type of interaction!) I talk to the person involved, and I say this:

'I'm not so much worried about the mistake. Mistakes happen. We make mistakes, too. What I'm concerned with is your *response*. What happens next? Your response needs to be immaculate. How are you going to use this to move forward to improve your best practice? What do we both need to do in order to ensure this doesn't happen again?'

Sometimes I ask them to put together a brief review document assessing their procedures. What went wrong? What are they going to change for next time? It's a reasonable thing to ask for – and it gets a good response. And suppliers that deal with me end up raising their game over time. My relationships with my suppliers have become strengthened. We know, like and trust one another.

## Partners who refuse to raise their game tend to fall by the wayside.

My own team has been trained to be immaculate, transparent, responsible. Sure, we make mistakes, but by golly, we jump on those mistakes and correct them immediately. We're committed to constantly developing our own best practice. We turn on a dime. We're always watching – always paying attention – always assessing – always tweaking. Our response time is blindingly fast. And people who work with us come up to that bar as well. Or we simply leave them, and find another supplier. Because the world is full of suppliers! How do you choose a supplier? I call it the Happy Factor. Work with people who make you happy and make you feel good. Butterflies eat nectar – not vinegar. You're a butterfly business. You're light. You're free. There are a million flowers out there – and a million suppliers. Try one. Assess their performance. Do they make you feel happy? No? Then Tweak. Get rid of them, and Try another one.

## Don't deal with people who leave a sour taste

If you're dealing with someone who's miserable and makes you feel miserable, and won't take feedback or raise their game – then, as we say in Wales, just jog on, Dai John! And land on another butterfly branch – one that's sweeter to the taste. You're offering a valuable contract – you're paying for a service or a product. Vote with your feet. Go and find the supplier who has values that mesh with your own.

Because... you're that cat. You do wonderful work, for wonderful pay. You supply the best to your own customers, and you deserve the best from your suppliers. You deserve the best from the world around you, and you can make the world a better place on your way through it. Insist on it!

# *Step* 10

# TAP IN TO YOUR
# HORMONAL SUPERPOWERS

How to turn your PMS into a superpower. The power
of resting. Harness the power of your hormonal
ups and downs with the lunar workflow.

A s women, we take a lot of flak for suffering from PMS. Jokes about it in the workplace are rife. But if you suffer from PMS yourself, you know it's no joke. The creeping sense of futility and despair... the exhaustion... the sudden hatred of everything in your life, even the things that were perfectly acceptable just the day before... the startling conviction that everything has been a massive waste of time.

You know what I mean. It's like putting on a pair of sh*&-tinted glasses, and all of a sudden, everything that was fine yesterday suddenly looks horrible to you, for no apparent reason.

So you may be surprised – and even delighted – to find that your hormonal cycling isn't a liability, Rather, if explored and harnessed properly, it can be a great gift. Yes, that's right – your hormonal cycle actually gives you superpowers! Lisa

Lister has written a great book about this, called *Code Red* – it's highly recommended reading. I've been inspired by her ideas and added in some of my own.

Note: if you're a man, or a menopausal woman, or a woman who isn't cycling because of birth control, etc., don't worry. This info does still apply to you. We're just going to work with the cycles of the Moon, instead of your own personal cycles. But the principles remain the same.

Human beings are more closely linked to the Moon than we realize, and the similarity between the words 'Moon' and 'month' is no coincidence. Each phase of the Moon – new, first quarter, full, and last quarter – occurs, on average, once a month. Scientifically speaking, the phases are dictated by the distance between the Sun and the Moon and the light visible on the Moon from Earth.

## The effect of the Moon on Earth

The four prominent phases of the lunar month – which occur roughly 7.4 days apart – are new Moon, first quarter, full Moon, and third quarter. As the position of the Moon changes in its orbit, the gravitational pull of the Moon on Earth changes and the amplitude of ocean tides also varies. Since the human body is 60 per cent water, it's not unreasonable to suppose that the Moon's changing pull might also affect us in varying degrees.

Science backs this up. Research, including 'Effects of Different Phases of the Lunar Month on Humans' by Ujjwal Chakraborty, details a large number of investigations that have shown the association of different lunar phases with the mental health or physical health and diseases, physical activity patterns and reproduction of humans.

What's certain is that paying attention to the Moon, with its phases of waxing and waning, offers a powerful metaphorical alternative to our modern you-will-definitely-burn-out option of trying to force yourself into high noon, all the time.

Women naturally move through hormonal cycles that echo the Moon's phases. The sooner you embrace those changes, instead of seeing them as a simple failure to burn bright all the time, the happier and more productive you will be.

## You're not inconsistent, my lovely – you're cycling.

No one wonders why the Moon isn't full all the time. We accept that the Moon needs to recede, withdraw and renew each month – and so do we. We travel across different emotional states the same way the Moon travels around the Earth. The more attuned we are to these phases and how they affect us, the better we can harness the different energies, rather than wasting more energy fighting against them.

## Re-establish contact with cycles of nature

If you stop to think about it, it's actually pretty crazy to imagine – as we seem to do in modern life – that everything should be bright light, high Moon, full sun and total productivity, all the time. I've come to believe that concept is a massive con, unloaded onto us by the purveyors of electric lights. Just because electricity means that we can work 24 hours a day,

7 days a week, around the clock and around the year without stopping or pausing – doesn't mean we should. We've lost touch with the natural cycles, the circadian rhythms of waxing and waning. We're mammals – we're animals. We lose touch with these rhythms at our peril.

As women, it's easier for us to re-establish contact with these natural cycles, because our bodies naturally wax and wane with the Moon. But men, as well as women who don't cycle, can acquire the same wisdom of privileged rest and extra strength, with a bit of extra attention. Turns out, we human beings have seasons, just like the planet does!

Here's how you can put those natural cycles to work for you:

### Phase: New Moon/Winter

### Focus: Resting, rebooting

If you're a woman who is cycling, your winter season begins with Day 1 of your period, and goes through to Day 7. This is the day you start counting from, going forward. And yes, this means you're going to have to keep track of your own personal cycle, and write it down. It's a great exercise – the more you know about your own hormonal life, the more empowered you'll be!

Hormonally, winter is the time that your oestrogen hits its rock-bottom levels, leaving you feeling achy and tired, and then begins a steady climb again. By around Day 3, your increasing levels of oestrogen will give you a mild boost in energy, optimism and brain clarity. When oestrogen rises, it also boosts your testosterone, which will give you slowly increasing feelings of confidence and courage. But these levels, while increasing slowly, aren't as high as they will be later in your cycle. Winter is the time to curl up, retreat into yourself, reboot and renew.

If you're not cycling, your winter period begins with Day 1 of the new Moon. Don't know when the new Moon is? Just google 'lunar calendar' and you'll find out where you are today, in the current Moon cycle.

Scientifically, the new Moon is when the Sun and the Moon are on the same side of the Earth. Because the Sun isn't facing the Moon, from our perspective on Earth, it looks like the dark side of the Moon is facing us.

Whether it's hormonal or lunar, your winter season should be a time of rest. It's not true that nothing is happening during winter.

## Winter is an important part of the year. Things are resting, refreshing, renewing.

It may look barren above ground – but below ground, there are things happening, preparing for future growth. You've got to gather your strength before you spring out again. Everything in your body pulses with a back-and-forth rhythm – your breath, your heartbeat – and your energy is the same.

In this culture we're terrific at focusing on the light, bright, achieving parts of the cycle – but we're really bad at relaxing into the dark, quiet parts of the cycle. Winter is about choosing isolation. It's about going into your room and closing the door.

Historically, it's when women took time away from others. This is your retreat period. It's time to reboot – a time when you can regain your strength to begin again. New beginnings, fresh starts and clean slates. And the beauty of it is that you get another brand-new fresh start every 28 days! Whatever has happened during the last period of time, let it go. It's time to start again.

## Treat yourself to some alone time

Try to envision yourself filling up – recharging under the energy of this new Moon. Unplug and treat yourself to much-needed alone time, without apology. You may find yourself feeling anti-social and introverted for no reason. Pay attention to these feelings and embrace them. Turn yourself inward and away from the draining energy of others. Don't feel bad for cancelling plans or not wanting to call, text or be around anyone. *No guilt!* Turning off is the best way to make the most of a new Moon.

If you're running your own business, you have the great advantage of scheduling some activities around your own personal seasons. Winter, for example, isn't the best time to schedule something extroverted like an exhibition, or an important meeting, or launching a new product. Your energy isn't out and about – you're curled in on yourself now. Try to use this time for things to which it's best suited – thinking, cogitating. Retreat behind closed doors with your journal and some dark chocolate. (70 per cent or higher cocoa solids, please! Your gut bugs will thank you.)

## Your new Moon/winter superpower: Clear-sightedness

Because you're lacking the 'bubble-me-along' hormones that keep you feeling optimistic during other parts of your cycle, this is the time to take a good hard look at things and see them as they really are. Anything that needs to be changed in your life will present itself for examination during this time. Take the information in. This is a time when you have the mental bandwidth for something new to be created. You'll know instinctively which direction is best for you to take in your life, moving forward. The new Moon offers a different kind of perception – in the darkness, we feel and sense our way forward. These ways of knowing are heightened at this time. You'll become super-clear about your purpose. Slow down and allow your intuitive self to provide you with insight and creative ideas. Your instinct is very switched-on during this time. Write down any ideas that occur but don't act on them – not yet. It's not time for action. Just for resting, evaluating, retreating from the world. If you feel emotional, let those waves wash over you – use the 'leaning in to emotion' exercise in Step 11. Practise saying, 'No', and being magnificently selfish. Cat B knows how to ask her family to run her a bath, bring her a cup of tea and a bar of dark chocolate, and leave them at the door!

---

## *Phase: Waxing Moon/Spring*

## Focus: Setting intentions

If you're cycling, this is Day 8–14 of your cycle. You'll be experiencing a steady increase in oestrogen levels, which boost serotonin levels. Serotonin is the communication neurotransmitter in the brain (and the gut) that allows one neuron to communicate with its neighbour. So as your serotonin levels rise, your levels of happiness, optimism and ability to communicate effectively are also on the up.

Your verbal abilities are on the increase, so this is a great time to make an important presentation or an important call. Memory, logic and creative skills are on the increase, as is physical energy and stamina. It's the perfect time for laying plans, setting intentions and planting seeds that will come to fruition later in the cycle.

Rising oestrogen levels also mean that you're able to overlook problems and issues with the people around you more easily than you would at other times in your cycle (hello, autumn and winter!) You're less likely to be oversensitive about being critiqued, so this is a good time to ask for feedback and put forward new ideas. You have more patience. As your testosterone levels increase, you'll feel a rising sense of security and confidence, so you'll be more adventurous and more able to try new things.

If you're not cycling, your spring phase begins on the 'first quarter' Moon and continues during the seven or so days when the Moon is 'waxing', or moving towards becoming full. The waxing Moon represents intention, hopes and wishes.

### After recharging under the new Moon, your new intentions and desires are ready to be planted. It's action season.

This is when you should be developing your intentions and laying the mental groundwork for your next project. Spring is an exciting time. You come out of your resting period like a racer out of the starting blocks, super-charged and ready to go!

## A time for new collaborations

Spring is a great time to schedule marketing and PR, start new collaborations. You'll want to start new projects now, and you'll feel that you can take on the world. You may find that you can get things done in half the time they normally take. Take advantage of your boundless energy now to write a bunch of blog posts that you can schedule throughout the month. Or do some batch cooking and put things in the freezer for autumn and winter. Your future self will thank you.

Just be careful that your boundless spring energy doesn't lure you into overcommitting yourself to projects that you won't want to fulfil, when autumn and winter come back around.

### Your waxing Moon/Spring superpower: Taking action

This is the time when you naturally open new brain loops and start new projects. Everything seems possible during this season. Now is the time to reach out and make new connections. Make plans. Set intentions. Take advantage of the natural energy that's shooting up. Think: challenges, decisions, and action. Be prepared to make decisions on the spot, and don't lose your cool when things come at you out of nowhere. Be flexible. Maximize your ability to see new potential during this period.

### Phase: Full Moon/Summer

### Focus: Performing, displaying, connecting

If you're a cycling woman, this is your ovulation period – your time to shine! Technically it can occur anywhere between Day 13 and Day 21 of your cycle. Everyone loves you, and you love everyone. It's a very high-energy time, when you can be all things to all people. Superwoman, look out, there's a new girl on the block! Since Day 1 of your cycle, your hormones have been conspiring to bring you to this very moment, one of peak fertility.

## You're feeling energetic and optimistic.

From an evolutionary point of view, your peaking levels of oestrogen and testosterone at this time combine to make you happily overlook the flaws or failings in the people around you – increasing the chances that you might want to breed with one of them! Optimism is the mood of the day. This also means it's a great time to collaborate, get along, and be your best sociable, expressive self.

If you're non-cycling, your summer period begins with the night of the full Moon and continues to the 'third quarter Moon'. A full Moon occurs when the Sun and the Moon are on opposite sides of the Earth. Because the Sun is directly across from the Moon, the light completely illuminates it, making the Moon appear completely full to us on Earth.

### Harvesting what you sowed

This is harvest time and time for you to reap the benefits of your intentions set during the spring. You'll see these benefits in the form of new opportunities or results from the hard work done in the previous weeks. Make sure you're prepared and open to receiving these. The themes surrounding this Moon are gratitude, sharing and enthusiasm. You should be feeling the benefits of your hard work for the last two weeks. Your metaphorical crops are in abundance. Now is the time you'll be feeling full of love, and you'll want to give back to those around you.

> ## This is time to show your stuff; the perfect time for an exhibition, a presentation, a dinner party, a demonstration.

You're in your full glory, confident and gorgeous. In our WATT group, we have a Full Moon Market, where everyone shows off their wares to one another. Your sense of self is strengthened, so you can get out there and shake your peacock tail feathers around! You look your best, feel your best and are harvesting the seeds that were planted during your spring season.

### Full Moon/Summer superpower: Reaping the rewards

This is the time when everything comes to fruition. All your winter resting and spring intention-setting – it all comes together during this period. Harvest all your hard work! You're at your peak. Try to schedule big events during this time. Hustle for new business – do meet-and-greets. Even if you normally feel a bit shy about your business, this is the time to really get out there, wave your flag and blow your trumpet. You're amazing, and it's time to let the world know it!

---

## *Phase: Waning Moon/Autumn*

## Focus: Editing and pruning

Now here's where the nitty gets gritty. This is the infamous PMS period, when your body is preparing for winter. Oestrogen and testosterone levels are dropping like a stone, along with serotonin. The lack of serotonin will be making you touchy, tired and possibly aggressive, or weepy, or angry. What could possibly be good about a time like this, you might wonder? Well, here's the good news – you become a brilliant editor during this period.

Think of oestrogen and testosterone as 'rose-tinted glasses' that keep you bubbling along and allowing you to overlook the problems in your day-to-day life. As mentioned, the evolutionary advantage to this is that you're much more likely to breed with a male in the neighbourhood if you're able to overlook his annoying little habits! So nature does you the great favour of pumping you full of these lovely mood-boosting body chemicals just at the point when you're most fertile. But afterwards – well, not so much. Once these optimistic, 'no-problem-he's-just-a-fixer-upper' hormones fade in your system, you're exposed to harsh reality – sans filters.

## Preparing for the future

There's a theory that if you grab hold of this reality each month, and investigate it, you'll be better prepared for menopause – which is the time when those rose-tinted glasses disappear forever. Better to fix your life in little monthly batches, as you go along, rather than continue to be bedazzled until it's too late – and you get whomped with ugly reality that you haven't fixed along the way.

If you're non-cycling, autumn is the time from the 'third quarter Moon' down to the new Moon. The themes here are 'release' and 'letting go'. The Moon is waning, gradually decreasing in size, and it's time for you to do the same – let go of whatever doesn't belong.

During the past month, while you've been setting intentions, taking action and displaying your harvest in the outside world, you've learned things. You've discovered things. You've accumulated things. Maybe you've been hurt, and you've sustained some dents and dings in the process. Now it's time to release all of that.

> **Surrender and purge yourself, get ready to rest and receive new intentions that you'll set again in the next cycle.**

A great practice during this Moon is a cleanse. Clean out your apartment, your closet, your friendships. Look at anything that's no longer serving you and get rid of it. Pay attention to the unnecessary emotional and physical clutter you've accumulated during this past cycle and rid yourself of it. Time to clear the decks!

### Waning Moon/Autumn superpower: Clearing the decks

So, this is the joy and the gift of autumn. You can edit. You're ruthless at this time, because anything that doesn't fit is hugely irritating to you. Out it goes! It's a great time to clean up and clear out, an ideal time to declutter. In fact, don't even waste your time trying to declutter during any other season – because you're so magnificent at it during this time.

My husband and my son know all the signs. 'Autumn!' they groan when I come down the stairs like a cold wind and suddenly start asking leading questions, like why on earth are there five hammers and 17 pairs of wellies sitting in the front porch? These are things that my eyes slid over acceptingly only the day before – but suddenly, their presence there is unbearable.

That's the joy of autumn. You transform into the mighty super-broom, come to sweep all the mess away. Cobwebs, beware. Take your power at this time and use it for an almighty muck-out. Side note: You also become an incredible human lie detector. No one can get anything past you. Old relationships, outdated beliefs, mismatched crockery – out they go!

And once you've cleared out and released, the slate is clean and we're ready to retreat into ourselves, rest and recharge again under the new Moon.

---

## A fresh start is always just around the corner

This cycle is never-ending, repeating every 28 days. I love this idea because it contains so many fresh starts – and I love, too, that there's a sacred blueprint for action here! Clean the slate, rest, set an intention, act on it, harvest the results, feel grateful, release whatever isn't needed, surrender, begin again.

Each cycle of action is like the spiral of a conch shell – not going around in meaningless circles, but building, one upon the next, so that you create your own beautiful holding.

You create your own conch as you move forward – and when one life compartment becomes too small for you, you'll create a new one and move into that. This is how you create your life, your work, your business.

If you're interested in bringing the lunar workflow concept into your life, it couldn't be easier. Just look up 'Moon phases' online, and find out where the Moon is tonight. Then once it gets dark, go outside. Take a chair, make yourself comfortable and do a little 'Moon bathing'. Sit quietly, whether or not you can see the Moon, and meditate a bit about what the current phase can teach you right now. How does it apply to your life? What can you learn from it? How can you sink into it? How can the lunar workflow support you? Capture these insights in your journal.

# *Step* 11

# LEAN IN TO
# YOUR EMOTIONS

---

**Handling your emotions skilfully can be the
key to unlocking your business's potential.
Here's what you need to know. Why you
shouldn't leave all emotions at the door.**

---

I magine for a moment that life is a school, and that every event that occurs during your day, good or bad, is your assigned curriculum.

Imagine that every time something happened to you, you leaned towards it, felt the feelings it brought up in you, pulled it towards you, learned any lessons it had to teach you, and moved on.

Imagine how smoothly and quickly you'd move.

Imagine how you'd get out of your own way.

Imagine how little you'd fear.

Imagine how little time you'd waste trying to avoid feeling pain.

Imagine the things you'd accomplish, the places you'd go, the emotion you'd feel, the people you'd help.

I'm going to make a suggestion here:

Try believing it.

If life really is a school, and every event is your curriculum, and you start actually behaving that way – great. You're doing what you're here to do.

And if it's not true – well, there's no downside. You're going to get a whole lot more out of your life: suffer less, progress faster. And who knows...

Maybe it *is* true!

## The problem of pain

Here's the thing – we spend most of our time trying to avoid pain. We do this in any number of ways: alcohol, sugar, drugs, shopping, gambling, pornography, food, Internet or TV. Which is your own personal favourite?

When something bad happens, you want to turn away from it – because it hurts. That's fair enough. It's instinctive. That's what animals do – if you hurt them, they flinch from the pain. It's part of the hard-wiring system that's designed to keep us alive.

But here's the challenge – in the modern environment, a lot of our biochemical reactions are simply obsolete. Remember our discussion about the increasing pace of change? The world around us has changed faster than our biology. We simply haven't evolved fast enough, physically, to keep pace with our modern surroundings.

## Now that our biology is outdated, we're often hard-wired to get it wrong.

For example, we still automatically respond to a perceived threat with an adrenaline reaction that robs all the blood from the language-processing centre of our brain and sends it to the large muscles in our arms and legs. It made perfect evolutionary sense, back in the day. If a tiger is attacking, you don't need to talk – you just need to fight, or run.

But that strategy doesn't work so well when we're standing in front of an audience trying to make a speech, and we go completely blank because there's no blood in the language centre of the brain! The nature of the challenges facing us has changed, but our HPA axis (hypothalamic-pituitary-adrenal axis) still behaves the same.

## Overriding the automatic response

Here's the good news, however – we're not completely at the mercy of our obsolete biology. Sure, we're still hard-wired to retreat from emotion or physical pain. That's our reptilian brain at work. It's kept us alive for eons.

But these days, we also have our forebrain with which to work. Beautiful, elegant, perched like a scoop of ice cream on top of the old reptilian brain – our forebrain enables us to choose. This lovely little addition gives us the option to override our automatic biological response. It's possible – although not easy – to select or modify our reaction to pain. It's possible for us to choose our behaviours. We don't just have to go along with our animal programming any more.

As a result, as set out beautifully in the book *The Better Angels of Our Nature: A History of Violence and Humanity* by Stephen Pinker, we're now actually less violent than at any time during history. Our young men still feel the aggressive urges of testosterone running in their system – but in many places around the world, they work this out on the rugby pitch or the football field. Still wearing national colours – still struggling against one another – but wielding a ball instead of swords and spears.

That's progress.

## A workout for your emotions

So here's some more progress for you – I'm going to suggest that you begin to lean in to all the experiences in your life, both painful and pleasurable, and pull them towards you.

This is exactly like the gym. You don't love those weight machines, do you? But they're there to make you stronger. You lean in to them, you pull them towards you. Does it hurt? Sure it does. But as they say in the fitness world: no pain, no gain.

Putting your boots on the road when you run your own business is exactly the same. You're going to do the same thing, for exactly the same reason – because it makes you fitter. Stronger. More resilient. Gives you more energy. Makes you enjoy life more.

No one ever built up fitness by turning
their back on exercise. And no one ever
succeeded in life by spending all their time
trying to avoid painful experiences.

It's a bit like signing up, and paying for, an expensive university
– and then failing to attend any of the lectures. The professors
aren't going to come and get you. You're perfectly free to
spend your entire time drinking, partying and wasting time,
and avoiding going to class. Chasing pleasure and avoiding
pain.

But – the time you're wasting is your own.

So get ready to lean in. This process is really simple – but also
quite difficult, because it's exactly 180 degrees opposite what
we normally do, by both nature and design.

We're programmed to turn away from pain, and in fact get as
far away from it as possible. I'm now going to suggest that
you do exactly the opposite – I'm going to suggest that you
turn towards your pain, and actually inhale it straight into your
chest.

Crazy, right?

*I'm not doing that*, you may be thinking. If it hurts, why would
I want to inhale it into the centre of my heart?

## Avoiding our emotions makes them stronger

Here's the thing – it's the fastest way through. A study from the
University of Texas found that when we avoid our emotions,

we're actually making them stronger. This can create many maladies in the body and in the mind, causing a myriad of health issues.

Research suggests that suppressing emotions is associated with higher rates of heart disease, as well as autoimmune disorders, ulcers, IBS (irritable bowel syndrome), and gastrointestinal health complications.

**Whether you're experiencing anger, sadness, grief or frustration, pushing those feelings aside actually leads to physical stress on your body.**

Studies show that holding in feelings has a correlation to high cortisol – the hormone released in response to stress – and that cortisol leads to lower immunity and toxic thinking patterns. Over time, untreated or unrecognized stress can lead to an increased risk of diabetes, problems with memory, aggression, anxiety and depression.

Trying to avoid digesting your emotions can lock you into a fight-or-flight response, just as undigested food can lead to indigestion. Something triggers an emotional response, and suddenly you might start to obsess about all the things that are negative and convince yourself the most terrible consequences that could happen, definitely will happen.

This triggers your body's stress response and pushes you into a state of high arousal. That's when the cortisol spikes. A chemical called norepinephrine is triggered that raises your heart rate and blood pressure. You can get so keyed up that you can't slow down enough to understand the situation fully. The blood disappears from your frontal cortex. You don't take the time to see if you interpreted the stressor correctly, because you can't – there's no blood in the logical centres of your brain!

## The difference between pleasure and happiness

Ultimately, you can't avoid your pain. Engaging in behaviours designed to avoid or push it away (drugs, shopping, alcohol, food, sex, Internet, gambling, etc) only create more pain over time. Avoiding pain and pursuing pleasure ultimately doesn't lead to happiness. Biochemically, it can't.

And here's why:

There's a difference between pleasure and happiness.

Aren't they the same thing?

No, they're absolutely not. As endocrinologist Robert Lustig explains in his book, *The Hacking of the American Mind: The Science Behind the Corporate Takeover of Our Bodies and Brains*, pleasure and happiness are two completely different things, biochemically speaking.

### Knowing the difference between pleasure and happiness could change your life forever.

Pleasure is created by a chemical called dopamine. Dopamine creates a 'reward-generating' pathway in your brain that delivers the same sensation of pleasure, no matter what the source of pleasure is. Pick your stimulus. It can be an activity, like shopping, gambling, watching pornography or surfing the

Internet. It can be a food – sugar is a classic. It can be alcohol, or drugs. Whatever the source – the dopamine-pleasure kick produced is the same.

The problem? Dopamine is a 'poisoned chalice' substance – that means the more you get, the more you want. It's an excitatory neurotransmitter, and too much of it is neurotoxic – meaning that over time, it causes cell death. When dopamine is released, and the neuron on the other side accepts the signal, it can damage that neuron. To protect itself from damage, the neuron receiving the charge quite sensibly decreases the number of its receptors. (If you were a neuron, you would too!)

Result? Fewer receptors on the receiving neuron means that the dopamine has less effect. Every time you get a 'hit', or rush of dopamine, the number of receptors decreases. As a result, you need increasingly larger doses or 'hits' to get the same rush. Eventually, you end up with 'tolerance' – a state where even a large dose produces no effect. Once the neurons start to die off, you're a full-blown addict.

## Why sugar is never the solution

One quick and easy way to stimulate dopamine? Sugar. That's why you may reach for a chocolate bar when you feel down, imagining that it will give you a boost. Neurochemically, however, this is impossible. Sugar will give you a temporary dopamine pleasure rush, but it will never, ever – for reasons that we'll discuss shortly – make you happy.

Then if you add the stress hormone cortisol to the mix, you downregulate serotonin even further. What do you get then?

Addiction and depression. Look around any city in the world, and you'll see this illustrated in more ways than you can count.

It takes up to three weeks for the dopamine receptors to repopulate.

If you're really addicted, the cravings can go on for more than a year.

Now let's talk about serotonin. Whereas dopamine causes pleasure, serotonin causes happiness, or contentment. Serotonin isn't an excitatory neurotransmitter. When serotonin acts on its receptor, no damage occurs. So happiness, or contentment, doesn't lead to addictive behaviour.

But here's the real kicker: dopamine downregulates serotonin. So the more pleasure you have, the less happiness you're going to feel – and the more hits you're going to need, just to keep the pleasure level up.

**This means that it's basically impossible
to achieve lasting happiness (serotonin)
by engaging in pleasure-seeking
behaviour (dopamine.)**

Add to this the fact that to make serotonin you need an amino acid called tryptophan.

Tryptophan is like a teenager without a car – it has to ride-share its amino acid transporter with two other common amino acids: phenylalanine and tyrosine. What do these two amino acids do? They're precursors for dopamine.

Uh-oh. You see where I'm going here. Meanwhile, the more processed food you eat, the more dopamine you'll make, because processed food contains the ingredients for dopamine – so that's what gets made. Not that nice, lovely, sustainable serotonin that makes you happy in the long run. (This is why processed food is so addictive, by the way.)

You can't have both dopamine and serotonin – they compete for resources and cancel each other out. You have to choose. This is why addicts aren't happy people. Explains an awful lot, don't you think?

Pleasure seeking – dopamine behaviour – is a solitary thing. It tends to happen in isolation. Happiness – serotonin behaviour – is communal. It happens when you connect with others. People can make you happy and increase the amount of serotonin in your system. You can make yourself happier.

## How to forge the four habits of happiness

There are four ways to make yourself happy by boosting serotonin, according to Lustig. Most of them involve other people:

### Connect

Make genuine human connections. Turns out that Facebook doesn't count as connection. Interpersonal connection means eye to eye. The facial emotions of the person to whom you're speaking activate a set of neurons in your brain called mirror neurons, which are the drivers of empathy and specifically linked to serotonin. This doesn't happen online. In fact, just the opposite: social media generates dopamine – which leads to addictions – and reduces happiness. So online connection is another 'poisoned chalice' solution that ends up driving unhappiness.

## Contribute

Be part of something greater than yourself; make a contribution to society. Science shows that volunteering improves depression, life satisfaction and well-being, and results in a 22 per cent reduction in risk for death.

## Cope

Lack of sleep, insufficient exercise and multi-tasking are all causes of unhappiness. Sleep is very important for healthy serotonin production. Avoiding exposure to electronic screens is important as blue light inhibits melatonin production, making it harder to sleep.

## Cook

Eat real food that you prepare yourself. If you cook, you're most likely going to increase your tryptophan, reduce your refined sugar intake and increase your omega-3 fats (anti-inflammatory) and fibre. Overall, this benefits your gut bugs, which is going to increase serotonin. And cooking is often a communal activity, which can involve other people – a win-win on the serotonin scale.

---

Another win-win is recognizing and working with your own emotions. And your business is the perfect place to practise!

## The role of emotion in business

Imagine the typical CEO of a Fortune 500 business. What emotions would you associate with this person in the course of a typical day? What emotions would you imagine that he or she would express, or permit, in the workplace?

When I ask my team this question, they say: 'Aggression. Anger. Power. Dominance. Intimidation. Irritation.'

It's hardly a full, rich spectrum of human emotions, is it?

We've long associated emotion with being weak, unprofessional, feminine. You're told to leave your emotions at the door. As a young reporter, when I was upset over receiving some hate mail, and I went to ask my female boss for advice, she said, 'Get a thicker skin.'

'Businesslike' is the term commonly used as the antithesis of emotional. 'Strictly business'. 'It's just business' is a phrase often used to justify some horrific betrayal or other.

And yet... and yet...

Emotions are how I turned a £1 million profit in three years, from a standing start, with no business experience and no advertising budget.

Why? Because when it comes to emotions, until now, business has got it all wrong. Literally, 180 degrees, exactly upside-down, wrong.

Here's the pivotal piece of information that's been missing from the equation...

## Emotion is the major driver of human decision-making.

This is the dirty secret of the human brain – you make your decisions not on the logical side of your brain, but on the emotional side. The logical side of your brain can build up arguments all day long, but the actual moment of decision comes from the emotional side – the side that deals with humour, colour and narrative.

## User manual to the brain

Scientists know this because of the ground-breaking work of Antonio Damasio, a neurologist. Damasio worked with a successful attorney called 'Elliot' who underwent surgery on the right side of his brain to remove a tumour. While Elliot was able to function normally in many ways after the surgery, he could no longer make even the simplest decisions. The arguments would stack up endlessly – but the magical moment of choosing would never occur. It couldn't – because the emotional side of his brain was damaged.

You may reason and make pro-con lists all day long – but at the end of the day, it's the emotional side of your brain that drives you to actual action. That's how decisions are made.

I'm amazed at how little Damasio's research has percolated into our group consciousness. Yet this is mind-blowing, life-altering, game-changing information. This is the user manual to your brain, and the brain of everyone around you. The science is out there. And yet no one has applied this information to business – until now.

## *Acknowledging and harnessing our emotions*

Normally, human beings avoid emotion. We avoid it as much as possible in our day-to-day life, and we definitely avoid it in business. We particularly try to avoid negative emotions. We'll do *anything* we can not to feel these emotions – drink, take drugs, shop, watch TV, gamble. Addictions are largely fuelled by this desire to avoid negative emotions.

> ## So here's a radical, revolutionary, scary concept – what if you were to turn towards your emotions? Lean in to them, and pull them towards you, like weights in a gym?

I call this *'emotion recognition'*. This is the practice of leaning in to your emotions, instead of trying to push them away. Like anything, it's a discipline. You work it like a muscle.

What if you were to encourage the people around you to do the same? What if when a child felt sad, instead of saying 'Cheer up, don't cry,' and offering a cookie (hello, incipient food addiction...) you said, 'You know what? That *is* sad. I'd feel sad too.' And just sat there, offering your support while the child worked his way through and processed his emotions.

## Confronting and working with your own feelings

What emotion recognition means, ultimately, is that emotions are okay. It's okay to have them, and it's okay to feel them. In fact, you *need* to feel them, for the sake of your own emotional well-being.

### How to use emotion recognition on yourself

Imagine that you're turning directly towards the emotion. Take a moment to perceive it. Does it have a colour, weight, shape? Is it sharp or dull?

Then inhale that emotion straight into your heart. It may seem counter-intuitive and crazy, but it won't actually harm you. Just suck that painful feeling straight into you.

Then pause for a moment to think of all the other people in the world who are feeling exactly the same thing as you are right now – and breathe out peace, for yourself and for everyone else. Repeat this procedure three times.

---

This process allows you to assimilate your emotions so that you can absorb them – just as you chew up food, in order to digest it. Same process.

Here's an example of how this works:

Sh*& happens. Maybe you've had a conversation with a friend who has let you down. 'Sorry, I know we were going to meet up, but I'm just feeling really rough tonight.' You know it's an excuse. You're angry. You have the impulse to go online, to distract yourself. Maybe pour yourself a big glass of wine first.

Try this instead. Close your eyes and in your mind's eye, turn so that you're facing towards your anger. Now this is exactly 180 degrees opposite to what we're accustomed to doing – and even what we want to do.

> **Usually we want to avoid pain, and you're now going to be leaning closer to it. Turn directly towards it and breathe the anger straight into your heart. Sounds crazy – but try it.**

Breathe the anger into your heart. Pause at the top of the breath and think for a moment of all the millions of people out there who are feeling the exact same thing, at this very moment. Then breathe out – 'peace' for yourself, as well as for all those other people.

Now check in with the feeling. Has it changed, shifted in any way? Before it was, say, anger – maybe now it's changed to a feeling of frustration.

*She always does this to me. How stupid of me to get caught out again.*

So now breathe that frustration straight into your heart. Pause at the top of the breath to connect with all the millions of people feeling just exactly the same way as you, right this minute, and breathe out 'serenity', for yourself and for all of them as well.

Check the feeling again. Maybe it's softened now, to sadness.

*Why does this always happen to me? Alone again.*

Same again – breathe the sadness in, pause at the top to think of everyone else who's feeling the same thing, and then breathe out 'strength', for yourself and for everyone.

Keep doing this, pausing to check in with the feeling and identify it as it shifts, and then breathe in the new feeling. Carry on with this until what you're feeling is calm.

## Don't leave your feelings at the door

You can practise emotion recognition with the people around you, as well. Instead of trying to 'cheer someone up', or fix the problem, try just reinforcing their experience.

'Wow, that *is* really sad. I'd feel sad too.'

If the person is a child, help them find a word for the emotion they're feeling. Then just sit with them while they feel it. That's it! Simple. But incredibly difficult at the same time, because it's exactly the opposite of what we're used to.

I use emotion recognition in every aspect of my business. We don't ask our employees to leave their emotions at the door – we instruct them to bring those feelings with them. It's about authenticity. In our morning team meetings, everyone reports on how they're feeling, and gives the highs and lows of the previous day. It's like an emotional weather report.

This might sound a bit touchy-feely-airy-fairy, as my pragmatic Welsh farmer hubby might say. But it has a real bottom-line impact on our team alignment. If someone's grandmother has died, or father has been taken to hospital, or dog has been hit by a car – it matters. It impacts that person's emotional state, and they're going to be carrying it around all day. The team members with whom that person works will be registering that emotion at some level and wondering what's going on.

Because human beings are constructed the way we are, we always project the worst possible outcome onto a blank screen.

> ### If someone doesn't tell you what's wrong with them, you're going to assume something – usually the most negative possible outcome.

Frequently, people blame themselves. 'She's acting strange today – is it me? Did I do something wrong? She's angry at

me? Why? Maybe she's cross that I took the last tea bag...'
And on and on. Endless confusion, and everyone getting
crossed wires in the workplace.

It's so much simpler if we all know that someone on the
team has suffered a personal loss or a setback. We can
offer them cups of tea and a bit of extra sympathy. Maybe
their manager will check in on them, see how they're doing,
offer them the opportunity to leave early that day. This kind
of knowledge sharing leads to intimacy and alignment on
the team. People feel part of the platoon – we're all in it
together. We look after one another. We stay current with
what's happening to everyone. To me, it makes the most
hard-headed business sense.

## Dispelling the myths

To summarize, let's explode some long-held and cherished
beliefs about emotion in business:

1. Emotion has no place in business.

   **Wrong.** Decisions are made on the emotional side of the
   brain. Customers buy from brands they know, like and
   trust. It's *all about emotion.*

2. It's unprofessional to show emotion in the workplace.

   **Wrong.** Displaying emotional authenticity in the workplace
   both brings a team closer together and creates unshakable
   alignment – the holy grail of management.

So go forth, and be emotional!

## *Step 12*

# WHAT TO DO
# WHEN THINGS GO
# HORRIBLY WRONG

---

**Your crisis survival toolkit.**
**The only question you ever need to ask.**

---

When things go wrong – and oh, my lovely, things will go wrong because that's just the nature of boots on the road – here's what you need to know.

There are only 4 elements to every event:

1. How you feel about it.

2. What you can learn from it.

3. How you're going to respond to it.

4. How that event moves you forward.

So, the first step is to feel your feelings, as discussed in the previous chapter.

## Breathe in – feel that emotion

We begin with breathing in the emotions because before any work can be done, you have to process the raw feeling. Luckily, you come ready-equipped with the perfect tool for that – your heart. Your heart is an organ of assimilation, designed to digest and process emotion, just the same way that your gut is an organ of assimilation designed to digest and process food.

We're very accustomed to the idea of processing food – but we're not very good at processing emotion. We don't know how. And we don't want to. And somehow there's an odd belief that all emotions should all be pleasant emotions. If the emotion isn't pleasant, then we simply try to avoid it, in any number of ways.

The challenge with that is that it's like saying, 'If the food doesn't taste sweet, I'm not going to eat it.' It simply doesn't work that way. Not all food is sweet. Food tastes all kinds of ways. And you can't simply refuse to ingest food that isn't sweet. It's not healthy. Neither is turning away and trying to avoid any emotion that's not pleasant.

You've got to turn towards that emotion, breathe it in, assimilate and digest it.

> The events in your life, and the emotions
> they precipitate, make up your curriculum.

They're your experience. That's the grist for your mill, your own unique, particular and individual life. It's your material, and every minute you spend trying to avoid experiencing it, is as much a waste of time as if you paid for an expensive university education, and then refused to attend any of the classes. The time you're wasting is your own.

Suck that emotion straight into your heart, think of everyone else who's feeling just the same way right now, and breathe out peace for yourself and for everyone else. Watch for the subtle ways that the emotion shifts. Breathe the new feelings into your heart. Repeat until you're feeling calm. Following this process means you won't be avoiding or stuffing down your feelings – you're chewing them up and assimilating them fully.

Once you've processed the emotions, then it's time to squeeze the learning juice from the event orange.

## Ask: How is this an opportunity?

Once you've digested your feelings, you're ready for Phase 2 – the brain bit. For this you're going to need your notebook and a pen.

I'd like you to write down and answer this question: 'How is this an opportunity?'

If you only take one thing from this book, let it be this question. Asking this question consistently is a high-performance pattern. Write it on the front of your journal. Pin it to the wall. Tattoo it on your bicep.

Tell this to the people around you, and ask them to remind you when you're too lost in the depths of despair to remember it yourself. My 14-year-old son has this one down to a tee. Right when I'm sunk in the folds of some terrible crisis, he'll pipe up, 'How is this an opportunity, Mum?' I want to throttle him in those moments. But it also makes me laugh – and think. And sure enough, there's always a good answer to that question. It jars me out of my stuck position.

This is how we move forward. It's how we proceed.

**It's how you convert the stones that life
is throwing at you into building materials
for your own personal castle.**

Sometimes in the middle of a crisis, when you ask yourself the question 'How is this an opportunity?', your brain will just snarl back, 'It isn't.' Then you have to persist with yourself. 'Well, if it were an opportunity, what would the opportunity be?'

Keep working with this one, and you'll find that everything is an opportunity. Even the really bad things. Especially the bad things. They're the very events that rip our carefully constructed boxes apart at the seams and catapult us out into a new reality. When energy like that comes along in your life, go with it. A tsunami wave only takes you down if you run away from it. Try surfing it, instead. You might find out that it takes you exactly where you need to go.

### How we handled a curveball

Let me give you an example, a very recent one. It shows a little bit how one crazy thing can lead on from another:

Because our unsweetened kefir tasted so tangy, I had to educate people on its health benefits in order to sell it. Because of that, I got fascinated by the topic of gut health and ended up writing a few books on the subject. Because I was constantly researching for my books, I sat up straight in my chair the moment I saw a home microbiome test hit the market. I knew it was brand new science, and I wanted to get it to my clients, ASAP.

Since the lab provided results in a 70-page PDF report that I knew would melt everyone's eyeballs, I decided to sell my tests accompanied by a free nutritionist appointment with a nice human being who would explain everything. I advertised for a qualified nutritionist – there weren't that many in my area – finally found one, hired him and then launched the tests for sale. People went mad for it: we sold over 400 test kits in the first week.

Then my nutritionist walked out on me.

Really?!!! Because I've got 300 customers who are expecting to talk to you, mate!

So I wept. I gnashed my teeth. I dutifully drank my G&T. And then I grabbed my own hair, pulled my own head up off the table and asked those two magic questions.

## What do I know now that I didn't know before? And how is this an opportunity?

Well, what I knew now was that my customers were really, truly hungry for the high tech of good science to tell them what was going on inside their gut – plus the 'high touch' element of someone to explain it to them. I was going to need a lot of nutritionists, to help all of them.

And how was this an opportunity?

## The first step out of the crisis

I was sitting out in the sun talking it all over with my trusty website designer, Han. (Our business is 100 per cent online, so instead of paying the overheads for a shop, I pay my website designer to stay on-site, within arms' reach, all the time. Worth every penny.) We live in a rural part of the world, and I was despairing over how I'd ever recruit enough nutritionists to help. And he said: 'We do everything better in-house, anyway. Why don't you just train the people who are already here to be nutritionists?'

Eureka! He's a genius, my website designer. So that's what I did. I offered every single person on my team, in every department, the opportunity to train as a nutritionist.

Five of them took it up. I thought I should probably train myself as well. So ultimately, I sent six members of the team – including myself – to nutritionist training school. I paid the (admittedly eye-wateringly high) cost of the multiple trainings, and gave each trainee dedicated work time to study and a computer to work on. One office assistant manned the phones while the other one studied, and then they switched. Same in the soapery, and so on.

## An investment in the future

Sure, the daily business stuttered a bit with so many bodies out at one time, but we survived. It was an investment in our team (our most valuable asset) and the future of our business (because as events have taught me, you can never have too many nutritional advisors!). They all took the final test, and everyone passed with flying colours.

What a win. Everyone ended up with an official qualification, which they all loved. It provided further education, goals and inspiration for the team. And I had a rocking group of nutritional advisors – which helps the customers, improves our service and looks great on the website. It completely changed our value proposition. And, probably, the future direction of the business as a whole.

So you see, that original wanger of a nutritionist quitting on me and throwing me under the bus was actually a blessing in disguise. What looked like a crisis was actually the best thing that ever happened to my business.

And the same is true for you.

> **Don't dread bad things happening.**
> **Don't hang back for fear of it.**
> **Bad things will happen, and that's okay.**
> **That's a good thing!**

Each obstacle, each hurdle, each disaster along the way is an opportunity for you to grow, stretch your legs, discard old assumptions and get shunted into a faster lane where you can be even truer to your gift.

And that, my lovely, is all I know about best practice. Just let life teach you what you need to know. Get out there with high hopes and be prepared to get bashed around. You don't have to be perfect – you just have to be brave enough to put your boots on the road!

I'm with you all the way.

## Step 13

# HOW TO MAKE
# THE RIGHT DECISION
# EVERY TIME

When you work for yourself, you're going to have
to learn to tune in to your Inner Boss – here's
how. Developing a 'surrender practice'.

In his book *Man's Search for Meaning*, Holocaust survivor
Viktor Frankl wrote, 'What a man actually needs is not a
tensionless state, but rather the striving and struggling for a
worthwhile goal, a freely chosen task.' I think he's in a pretty
authoritative position to talk about meaning, and when I read
this I realized abruptly that we've got in all wrong.

Somehow, we've had this idea that at the end of the rainbow,
if you do everything right, there will be eternal leisure. From
way back in the 1950s, there was this huge emphasis on
'labour-saving devices'. These days we continue barrelling
towards artifical intelligence as fast as we can, as if work is
a curse.

But just ask anyone who's just had their job taken away by a machine: the thing that creates happiness isn't actually eternal retirement and leisure. The thing that creates happiness is *good work* – productive, purposeful work that engages your heart, your mind and your soul, and makes you a productive and worthwhile member of the human race.

I once read a parenting book that said the best thing you could say to any child was, 'You're a great member of this team. What would we do without you?'

It's good advice for grown-ups, too. It's not enough just to do something you love (a hobby) or something you're good at (a passion) or something you can get paid for (a profession). It also has to be something the world needs. Your puzzle piece, to give you purpose and meaning, needs to fit into the larger puzzle. It has to be for something. That's what I mean by a 'heart-led business'.

And that something can't be money alone – or personal satisfaction, or status, or pleasure. We're group animals, we humans. Ultimately we'll live and die together.

> **It's time for you to join up with the tribe and contribute your bit, no matter how big or small that bit might be.**

Fifty years ago, economist Milton Friedman wrote in *Time* magazine what became known as the 'Friedman Doctrine'. He said that the social responsibility of a business is to maximize profit, and its only responsibility was to its shareholders.

I'm going to put it right out there – the guy was just wrong. The Friedman Doctrine has been to our planet what antibiotics have been to human health – a poisoned chalice. We've drunk that cup all the way down to the dregs – and look where it's left us.

So, since ideas are lighter than air and change can happen in a heartbeat, I'm going to make up my own damn doctrine. Why not? Milton Friedman doesn't have a monopoly on doctrine-making.

## A call to arms for business

I call mine the Heart-Led Business Doctrine, and it goes like this:

The social responsibility of a business is to be good from the ground up. That means it's:

- Good for the soil

- Good for the plants

- Good for the animals

- Good for the customers

- Good for the team

- Good for the business owner

- Good for the neighbourhood

- Good for the country

- Good for the world

Want to know why businesses have to be good from the ground up? Because it simply doesn't work, to rob one part of the ecosystem in order to benefit another. We're all connected. Deplete one section, and the rest will fall apart.

It's all a fractal, remember? A pattern that's the same, all the way up and down the scale. If you get your crystal right at the smallest level, your ice palace will be right as well. And if your original crystal is distorted – built on slave labour or torturing animals or destroying the planet – your ice palace will be flawed as well, no matter how big and grand it gets. The end never justifies the means. World War II taught us that.

## The secret is never to compromise. Never cut corners. Never sell out.

Don't get trapped by a big supplier into being forced to cut corners. Don't get yourself into so much debt that someone else can tell you what to do.

And don't forget the fifth circle of your own personal compass in Step 4 – the plan that the universe has for you, that mysterious wild card. Who knows where that will take you!

In my experience the universal bit has a particular – I dunno – fragrance to it. Things slip sideways, and then click together in a new pattern, which is better than anything you could have thought of by yourself, with your tiny human brain. More elegant, more perfect, opening possibilities you hadn't yet conceived.

When things come together in this way, I always feel a rush of excitement and a feeling of awe. It's like hacking your way through the jungle, and then suddenly floating up above the trees, and just for one magical moment, getting a glimpse of the whole damn awe-inspiring, breathtaking expanse of landscape. They don't last long, those moments, but, boy, are they precious!

## Surrender to the power of the universe

So, how do you get there? Paradoxically, you give up. Literally – you surrender. You can't think your way there, or plan, or struggle. You just have to surrender to the tide that's sweeping you along. Hint – the universe is going to have its way with you in any case, so you might as well surrender now. Makes everything a lot easier. Take the advice given to a swimmer caught in a riptide – thrashing around will make everything worse. Just relax and let yourself be carried.

And then? You ask for guidance. Put your hand over your heart, and ask it what you should do. Listen closely for your marching orders, and then do what you're told. It's a strange combination of complete surrender and total action.

It's not straightforward, and it doesn't stay done. It's an ongoing practice. So I do a five-minute meditation every morning, to keep me on the path. Remember, an aeroplane is off course 99 per cent of the time and yet still reaches its destination because the pilot is constantly correcting. So keep checking in with your heart-led intuition, and do what you're given to do that day. If you stop checking in and correcting, you'll soon find yourself waaay off course!

So here's the orientation meditation I use whenever I have a question to answer:

*I align myself with my heart.*

*I align my heart with the heart of the world.*

*I release all suffering and allow it to be replaced with joy.*

*I ask for guidance.*

*I offer surrender.*

There's a source of magnificent information that's close enough for you to touch. You have only to sit quietly and let it enter you. Don't panic. This knowledge is available to everyone, all the time. Open your eyes and come into your own classroom.

> **Stop asking what you expect of the world.**
> **Start asking what the world expects of you.**

I've found that everything takes practice. Mastery is a matter of subtracting muscle involvement, not adding it. As you get better at something, you use fewer and fewer muscles to accomplish the same action. This is why it's fun to watch anyone who's really good at something – they make it look easy. A great ballet dancer will look fluid and effortless on stage because they're actually using fewer muscles than a beginner.

That includes surrender.

## Seek guidance from within

I have a 'surrender practice'. What this means to me is that I spend a lot of time trying to get out of my own way.

If I don't have time to sit down and do the whole meditation, and I have something important to decide on the fly, I've developed a quick-use mantra. When I breathe in, I say: 'I ask for guidance.' And when I breathe out, I say: 'I offer surrender.'

I do this a lot.

I do it when I can't sleep (it works like a charm – nearly 100 per cent success rate). I do it before meetings.

Specifically, I do it when I feel overwhelmed. There are plenty of moments when I feel like 'Hell, how did I get myself into this situation?'

An example: Our business is innovation-based. What that means in practice is that there's no one to tell me what to do. Literally.

We make our kefir with real kefir grains. Grains are living organisms – they have seasons, they grow. One time they started disappearing. No one knew why, and there was no one for me to contact – no one in the UK has a kefir grain bank the size of ours.

I talked to my scientist friend at Aberystwyth University, who strained the grains for us. He didn't know. No one knew. We just had to figure it out.

So there are a lot of times when I have to depend on creating new systems, keeping our own records. Answering our own questions. Proceeding forward step by step, and feeling my way through.

> In a situation like that, I need all the logic
> that I have at my disposal – but I also
> need to navigate by the light of something
> bigger and smarter than myself.

That's when I turn to surrender.

I just think, 'Well, hell, I can't possibly handle this by myself.' But fortunately I don't have to! And then I practise surrender.

I can't tell you why it works – I can only tell you that it does.

Maybe it lowers my cortisol levels so that my own brain can function better. Maybe it allows me to feel connected to something bigger than myself, so that I make choices that are better long-term choices, instead of just short-sighted temporary ones.

Or maybe – and wouldn't this be nice – maybe we're all part of something bigger than ourselves. Maybe there really is a field of intelligence of which we're all a part. That's what the quantum scientists are telling us. And wouldn't it be great, to relax into that as if it were true?

## Practise listening to your intuition

One of the challenges of running your own business is that you're on your own. You have no one to ask, and no one to tell you what to do. It's all unfamiliar! From whom do you take directions now?

The fact is, you're going to have to get good at listening to your own intuitive voice. That's the quiet little voice that's often drowned out by the chaos of the world. This is where your morning routine comes in. You need to get aligned and centred. Your journal practice will serve you well in this process.

This process of aligning yourself with your authoritative inner voice is one of the most crucial things that you'll ever accomplish. Because honestly – whom do you really trust to be directing your activities during your one short, wild, precious life?

Your energy is your most important resource. Far more than your money, it's your life energy and it's precious and non-renewable. You need to be careful when you think about where to invest your energy and your time.

## You only have a certain number of days in your allotted span. What will you choose to do with them?

For my part, I was never lucky enough to have a boss that I loved and trusted enough to just carry on blindly following their instructions forever. But I wouldn't have chosen to leave my radio job, because it allowed me to make a good living for my children. So it was ultimately a good thing that I was sacked! Although it didn't feel that way at the time. That dramatic event pushed me down another life path, entirely. Thanks, universe.

## The brain's limitations

In any case, I ended up in a position where I needed to learn to listen carefully to my inner guidance. I'm also keenly aware of the limitations of my own brain. My brain has certain advantages – I can innovate products and spot holes in the marketplace. My journalist training gives me a sense of where the 'heat' is when something new comes along. But I don't have any business training, no business experience, and I'm hopeless at maths. I'm also extravagant, impulsive, lazy and not terribly practical. Not to run myself down – just being completely transparent with you here.

My brain has its limits. So whom can I trust, to tell me what to do? (Besides my husband and co-director, of course...)

Here's where surrender comes in.

It may seem counter-intuitive, but the further I get along my business road – and the more power I accumulate, the more money I have to play with, and the more dangerous and high-stakes my decisions become – the more I practise surrender.

It's my conscious intention to surrender more each day. It's the sole focus of my daily meditation. I'm not smart enough to figure everything out. And I don't want a tiny little business that will come from my tiny little brain.

> The most amazing things that have come about in my life have happened because I simply asked to be shown how to play my part in the universe's design.

My idea is that I'm the hands and the feet of the universe, and I ask to be shown each day how to proceed. The things that have happened to me as a result are extraordinary to the point of being miraculous – far more extraordinary than anything I could have thought up myself. It's really cool. And the more I surrender, the cooler it gets.

## Have faith in the universe

I've become a bit addicted to the process, if I'm honest. I love the uncertainty of turning myself over to the universe and not knowing what's going to happen next. Why would I opt for my own puny intentions, when I could go big with what the universe seems to have in mind for me? When I get really overwhelmed (which happens a lot!), I often find myself thinking, 'I can't possibly cope with this.'

And then I think, 'That's okay – because I don't have to. I'll just surrender it, and let the universe handle it.' And that's what I do. The universe has never failed me yet.

More full disclosure: even this far along the road, I'm still not entirely sure where I'm headed. And that's okay. My practice is to become more and more comfortable with the not knowing. I think that's called Basic Trust.

It's a funny thing – we recently hired an agency to handle our 'digital platform'. We're a long way now from the days when I did no advertising because I couldn't afford any. In the beginning I relied exclusively on social media because all I had to work with was the goats, the view and my own ability to tell a story. But then we hired these new advertising people, and they asked me to set 'targets'.

Hmm. I'm not really sure how to set targets. I never have. I'd never have been arrogant enough to set my sights on a 6000 per cent growth rate. Who would do that? That's crazy. And yet that's what the universe created for me when I stepped my puny brain back out of the way.

> So for me, it's always been less about the targets and more about listening carefully to that quiet voice inside me that tells me to go left instead of right.

That voice told me in the beginning that it was important that our goats be free-ranging, despite the fact that no one else kept them that way, and people told me it couldn't be done. And that same voice tells me today it's important that we switch to 100 per cent recycled plastic bottles, even though they're more expensive.

I'm asking the universe all the time – what do you have in mind for me? What should I do now, today? How can I best serve? What next? What now?

## Use your journal to piece things together

To make the most of that little voice in your heart, try examining the events of your day as if you were reading runes, or angel cards. What does each event mean? What can it teach you? What do you know now that you didn't know before? This process expedites your learning curve exponentially. Plus, it's really fun. This is what your journal is for – it's for prying the meaning and the learning out of the events of every day.

Think about your daily life as a collection of information that you can receive if you just ask. Then listen to the answer. That's how it works. It's just that simple.

Personally, I don't really set goals any more. It's not that I've become unambitious or complacent – far from it. It's just that any goals I might set for myself might not be the ones the universe has in mind for me – and I don't want to set myself off down the wrong track.

For me it feels more like a process of discovery. My intention is to discover what the universe wants me to do. How can I serve? What am I meant to do next? The quieter I can get, and the harder I can listen, the clearer those answers become.

The place that I receive that information is right over my heart – that bony central part right in the middle of my chest.

**I close my eyes, put both hands over that area of my chest, feeling the warmth, and breathe into my hands. When I do this, I can feel the awareness percolating down from my head, into my heart.**

Try it – it's a nice feeling. Most of us are up in our heads most of the time – and I think that's too high. If you want to do your thinking anywhere, your heart is a better bet than your brain. The heart emits an electrical field 60 times greater in amplitude than the activity in the brain, and an electromagnetic field 5,000 times stronger than that of the brain. The neurons within the heart enable the heart to learn and make decisions independent of the brain's cerebral cortex.

## The real heart of decision-making

I like to think of the difference between the brain and the heart as being like the difference between a calculator and a proper PC. Sure, the brain is a good little calculator and logic processor, but it's limited. In fact, it's limiting – one of the main functions of the brain is to limit the amount of sensory data we have coming in so we don't drive ourselves crazy. Like a limiter on a moped that keeps you from going too fast. Useful, but the brain's not the organ you want to turn to for making big, important decisions.

The heart, now, that's your real PC. Or, as I like to think of it – 'Personal Centre'. The heart is constantly taking in information processed by the brain, plus information gathered from all over the body, and from other people, and the surrounding energetic environment as well.

> ### Native Americans believe that the heart is the true physical seat of intelligence in the body, and I think they might be right.

Scientists have established that the heart communicates to the brain and the body via nervous system connections. Information is also passed via hormones produced in the heart itself, biomechanical information from blood pressure waves, and energetic information from the strong electrical and electromagnetic fields.

The electromagnetic field of the heart can be measured anywhere on the body (using an EKG with electrodes on the ankles and wrists) but it also exists for several feet outside the body. Activity in one person's heart can be measured in the brain waves of another person. The electromagnetic field of two individuals (both human or one animal, one human) who are touching or within a few feet of each other, can interact so that energy activity in the heart of one individual is registered in the brain waves of the other. The efficacy of touch for healing therapies may be due to this method of communication.

So I'm less interested in thinking up goals for myself in my tiny little personal brain and more interested in switching on the Personal Centre in my heart and taking instruction. I'm not big enough or smart enough to figure out what's going on, and what my part in it all is meant to be. But luckily for me – I don't have to be. I just have to sit there quietly, with both hands crossed over the centre of my chest. I align myself with my heart, dropping my awareness down to that space and enjoying the sudden quiet that occurs when my brain chatter stops. And then I align my heart with the heart of the world.

I ask what I'm meant to do next. Always ask.

I try to surrender. And then I prepare to work like hell.

## Getting your marching orders

It's a bit of a tricky business then, to balance surrender and activity. I try to stay prepared to throw the entire weight of my energy, action, and ability to accomplish behind whatever project it becomes clear that I need to focus on. I just don't always know what that project is going to be. Or why I'm meant to be working on it. The information kind of comes on a need-to-know basis – and apparently, I don't need to know a whole lot! It takes a lot of trust.

Surrender – to me, at least – doesn't mean sitting around and watching telly. It means having basic trust that the answers will become clear. It means that once you've received your marching orders, you march.

Remember we talked about the fact that there are beliefs that hold you back, and beliefs that pull you forward? My belief that I'm part of a universal design, that I'm playing my part, that I'm not responsible for everything, but that I'm responsible for my own patch, and that if I ask for help and guidance I'll receive it. Boy, these are beliefs that pull me forward. They leave me in a great place.

I don't feel abandoned. I never feel alone. And I don't feel that I have to handle everything myself. Which is a damn good thing, because I surely lack the capacity to do that! My tiny little brain just doesn't have the wherewithal.

**Luckily for me, the universe seems to have better plans in store for me than I could ever come up with for myself.**

And all I have to do is surrender to that and go along for the ride.

It's like the water ride in the amusement park. You know how you get into the little boat and they say, 'Please ensure that your arms and legs are inside the vehicle.' It's a lot like that.

So how about you? If you drop your awareness from your limiting brain down into your heart-based Personal Centre, what does it tell you?

What are your marching orders for today? And are you ready to march?

Surrender yourself to the universe's plan for you, and then keep your arms and legs inside the vehicle – because things are about to start moving!

# A FINAL THOUGHT

This weekend, I went for a walk with my two children in a 40-acre woodland that we'd just purchased with profits from our little kitchen-table business.

It was a beautiful sunny day. We hiked down the long valley, to the sound of birdsong, and paused at the bottom on a wooden bridge to look out over the river that runs through the woodland. Our woodland.

I was struck by the thought: 12 years ago, I was a single mother, escaping from an abusive relationship, with my two children and one suitcase in the back of my car. I was lost in a strange country with no money, no job and no place to live.

Five years ago, my new husband was deathly ill, and we had to sell his beloved motorcycle to raise money to buy packaging for our kefir. We couldn't afford to shop at the local shop for food – we lived on bowls of cawl (a traditional Welsh stew) made with big bags of potatoes from the farmer's market.

Today I'm standing with my children in an ancient woodland that we own.

It's hard to believe.

But I'm here to tell you that if you think you're trapped – *you're not.*

If you think you can't succeed – *you can.*

If you think it's impossible to change your life – *it IS possible.*

I know it is, because I've done it. And if I did it, *you can too.*

> ## Change can happen in a heartbeat.
> ## Your life is lighter than air – it's simply
> ## a construct of your beliefs.

So what's your dream? What do you want?

Write it all down. Write down everything. Dream some unreasonable dreams. Do you want more than enough money, so much money that you never have to worry? Do you want a house in France? A boat? A stable full of horses or alpacas? Write them all down. Be silly with it.

Be unreasonable. We've spent so much time being reasonable, being sensible, being told not to set our expectations too high. It feels vulgar, somehow, to dream big dreams. But here's the thing – dreams are free. Why restrict yourself? You can want anything in the world. It's not saying you're going to get it – but you can want anything at all, whether it's space travel or a million pounds, or world peace.

## The transformative power of dreaming

I did this exercise a decade or so ago, back when I was a single mother. On New Year's Day 2006, I packed my two children and one suitcase into the back of my car, and finally made my escape from the hell of an abusive marriage.

I remember driving into the deserted centre of the nearest town and parking on the side of the road. I listened to the silence. Even the children were quiet in the back seat. The town was empty, and I was utterly alone in a strange country, with few friends, no job and no money. Still, the peace and quiet was better than what I had left behind. I was glad to be free.

A year or so later, I was sitting at a bowling alley, supervising while my eight-year-old daughter had a birthday party with her friends.

I was alone – of course I was. Because I was a single mother, I was always alone. One of the most bitter things about being a single mother, I found, was the normal 'happy family' events where you'd expect to find a couple watching their daughter and her friends playing. But there was no couple – there was just me, trying to be enough, trying to do the emotional work of two parents on a tight budget. Lonely times.

But while the kids laughed and bowled, I was working and writing in my journal. I'd been listening to some Tony Robbins tapes (I'm a big fan of his, by the way; check him out if you haven't already) and he suggested this exact exercise – writing down a list of all the things you want, without limits.

Okay. Why not? I decided I'd do it. I took a deep breath.

## What did I actually want?

Well, first I wanted a partner. Someone kind, strong, loving, funny. Someone who adored children and animals, who would never, ever be violent or raise his hand to me or the children. I wanted my children to be safe and happy, to have a green and wonderful place to grow up. I wanted to live on a farm, on a hill, overlooking the sea. I wanted a lot of animals – with other people around to help take care of them!

I wanted a lot of money – millions and millions of pounds – enough that I'd never have to worry whether I had enough in my wallet to pay for the food and party bags or bowling shoes at my child's birthday party, ever again. Enough that I'd be able to buy my children whatever they wanted or needed. I wanted freedom. I wanted to be surrounded by a big, happy, laughing family. I wanted to live in an ancient stone farmhouse, where I'd feel safe. I wanted a job where I could be creative but also help people, where no one would tell me what to do, and I didn't feel that I was selling my soul every day.

When I was finished, I looked over my list and laughed at myself. Big dreams indeed, for a skint single mum sitting at a bowling alley.

But here's the weird part – that was just 13 years ago. And today, *I have every single thing on that list.*

I live in a 200-year-old stone farmhouse on a hill, looking out over the sea. I'm married to a kind, funny, strong man. He's a farmer, and he does indeed love kids and animals. We keep 50 goats – and we have a team of people to help us look after them. We run our own business. We bring in over a million pounds every single year. We have a big, happy, laughing family. And every day, I work at something I love that's all about helping other people, but also endlessly creative and exciting.

Not only did I get everything on my list – I got the details, right down to the sea view.

And that's the power of writing it all down.

## Commit your vision to paper

So write your list! What do you want? Write an entire list of all the things you want. Write each sentence this way: 'I want X. I want X.' Don't think too much about it. Be unreasonable.

Now I'd like you to go back and rewrite that list, like this: 'I choose X. I choose X.' Re-copy the entire list this way.

Now go back and reread it. See how it makes you feel.

Here's the thing…

> There's a tiny step between wanting
> and choosing. But that tiny step is like
> the tiny step between standing on the
> runway and stepping onto the plane.

*I want* is a child's statement. There's a little bit of petulance to it, and a fair measure of powerlessness.

But *I choose*? Now there's a different story. I choose means that you're exerting your intention.

Your heart is like a car. It can run dirty, on the fuel of pain and lack. Or it can run clean, on the fuel of love and joy and intention. And it's your choice. Literally – it's about what *you choose*.

Do you choose less plastic in the oceans? Do you choose a connected, loving life, with friends and family, and a safe place for your children and/or animals? Do you choose to run your own business? Then choose it. And release it. And wait to see what happens next.

## Learn to dream big

We're not particularly good at dreaming, because we haven't had a lot of practice. And we've never been taught how to do it properly. If we do it in school, we get told off. Ever heard these? 'Don't be silly.' 'Don't be stupid.' 'Stop wool gathering.' 'Pay attention.' and the ever-lovely, snotty, crushing, 'As if.'

But dreaming is a muscle – like anything, if you're going to get good at it, you have to exercise it.

Sometimes it's important to hold your vision in a warm, empty space, and just sit with it. Not race off immediately to try to put together a logical plan. But just make a date with your vision. Welcome it in. Sit still. And have a conversation with it. What does your vision want? What does it need? What is the first thing it would have you do?

This is what it really means, to start your own business. Because *your life is your business*.

> Your business – your entire life really – is an engagement between yourself and your vision. It's a back-and-forth interaction.

You don't have to come up with the solution from your own logical brain, you just have to ask the question and release it. And then listen. Oddly – and it does sound strange – your vision itself will provide the answer! If you just ask the question and press Send on the universal Google key.

Forget everything that you've been told about the way things *have to be*. The way that things *can be* is quite different, and that's limited only by your expectations. That's why, sometimes, proceeding with a logical, reasonable, sensible business plan can be a dangerous trap. Why predict logical growth that only comes in tiny increments? There's no room for magic there. Throw yourself open to the possibility of the splendid, the magnificent, the jaw-dropping. Very un-corporate, I know. But it can happen. It happened to me, and it can happen to you.

When is the right time to begin your new business?

Now.

But – but – but – (...I can hear you say...) I've got another project to finish first. I need to lose five pounds. Wait until the summer. Wait until the baby is older. My schedule will be lighter next semester, I'll start then.

B8((*(&^. Excuse my French.

## There's no perfect time to start your own business

The time to start is now because there will never be a perfect time. Or rather, now is as perfect as the time will ever be.

The perfect time is an illusion. It doesn't exist. It's like the concept of sterile. There's no such thing as sterile; there's just wiping out a lot of bugs to create an empty space into which the nastier bugs can leap. That's why kefir and probiotic skincare are better than antibacterial options – it's more effective to pre-emptively fill the space with good bacteria, which put the bad bugs back in their boxes.

It's better to pre-empt your fear and start now. The time to leap off the cliff is now, with your imperfect preparation and your half-baked ideas.

Why?

Because the perfect moment will never come. You're just stalling.

Because the journey will teach you as you go. The main thing you need is courage to jump off the edge.

## What's holding you back?

That voice in your head trying to convince you to wait until next September? That's your amygdala, bless it. The amygdala is a tiny, almond-shaped organ that sits deep within the brain. It's trying to keep you safe by preserving the status quo.

Your amygdala loves the way things are right now because familiar circumstances are easier to police. You know how it's difficult to sleep sometimes in a new environment, because you keep waking up with each unfamiliar new noise? That's your amygdala. It never sleeps. Its job is to keep you safe and to wake you up each time there's something it doesn't recognize. Your amygdala hates change because change makes it that much harder to keep you safe. When things change, everything seems scary because everything is unfamiliar.

Now, don't get me wrong. The amygdala is an amazing organ. When you start to step into the road and then instinctively yank your leg back in, just in time to avoid losing it, because a red sports car just swerved too near the kerb, that's your amygdala at work. If it was left to your forebrain, it would go something like this, 'Let's see, that's a 1967 Chevrolet Corvette L88 Coupé with side detailing and optioned with the L88 427 engine. Wow, it's got M22 4-speed, J56 heavy-duty brakes and...'

WHAM! You've just lost your foot.

The forebrain takes too long to process things. Immediate action to save your life, that's what the amygdala is for.

So, the amygdala does a great and necessary job of circumventing the forebrain and yanking your leg back to safety. But neither the amygdala nor the forebrain is the organ of choice when it comes to deciding when you should launch your new business. That honour goes to – you guessed it – the heart.

So sit quietly, with your hand over the bony bit in the centre of your chest. Drop your awareness down from your chattering brain to just under your hand. Relish the sudden silence as the brain chatter ceases.

> **And ask your heart when you should begin. The answer will be quick, decisive, instantaneous.**

And then act on it, as it's no use getting good advice if you don't action it.

Don't wait for perfection. This isn't the realm of perfection – nothing is perfect here. If we were perfect, we'd all be up doing cartwheels with the angels already. Nah, this is the level of messy, complete, half-baked, not-quite-good-enough. And that's okay. Develop a taste for that. And jump.

Remember, dreams are free. Dreams are lighter than air. And change can happen in a heartbeat. No dream police are going to come hammering at your door, demanding that you scale back your unreasonable dream, that it's creating noise and disturbing the neighbours. (Unless, you know, it is. But if so – they can just bl&$%* well get used to it!)

## Put your biggest, most beautiful dream out there

So dream unreasonable. Go big or go home. Never compromise. Never cut corners. Hold out for the whole burrito. It doesn't mean it will happen. But, hey – it doesn't mean it *won't* happen, either. One thing is for sure – if you do what you've always done, you're going to get what you've always had. And aren't you ready for something more?

So put your unreasonable dream out there. Make it big, and crazy. Write it on the page opposite. Colour around it with bright shades. Write it beautiful, and all we women in your sisterhood will hold the dream for you.

You go, girl.

We're with you, all the way.

Hugs,

*Shann*

# ACKNOWLEDGEMENTS

Thank you to Reid Tracey, the best publisher in the world, for his unwavering faith and support of me, Chuckling Goat and this book. Thank you to Michelle Pilley for editing me with such verve and insight, and thank you to Julie Oughton for her patience, flexibility and for being my plus-one at The Ritz! Thank you to Mary Conroy for her detailed copy-editing. Thanks to Jo Burgess for waving her magic publicity wand over me once again, and to the entire Hay House team – including Hannah Turner, Lizzi Marshall, Tom Cole and Leanne Siu Anastasi – I feel very lucky to be working with such brilliant people.

Thank you to my legendary agent, Bonnie Nadell, for believing in my books and taking such beautiful care of them.

Thank you to my beloved family: Ceris, George, Elly, Josh, Phia, Benj, Macsen, Isabella and Elis – you guys are my world. Thank you to my mother, Ann, for 'just trying it' with me, and for worshipping the imperfection!

Finally, thank you to my beloved husband and best friend, Rich, for all his encouragement, help and belief in me – and for finally teaching me the meaning of *perthyn*. *Caru ti.*

# ABOUT THE AUTHOR

Andrea Jones

**Shann Nix Jones** was the ultimate American city girl until she fell in love with a Welsh farmer at the age of 41. Shann and her husband, Rich, realized that they could do something extraordinary when they started to work with goats' milk and used it to heal their son's eczema, and Rich's life-threatening superbug infection. They decided to quit their respective day jobs, and try to make a go of the goats'-milk business full time. They now have 50 goats who have become like members of the family.

In April 2011, the couple launched their online business, Chuckling Goat, selling health-enhancing soaps, creams and probiotic kefir drinks, which they make by hand on the farm. The launch was a huge success, and today their award-winning homemade products are available in the United Kingdom and all over the EU.

**f** chucklinggoat

 @chucklinggoat

 @chucklinggoat

 info@chucklinggoat.co.uk

**www.chucklinggoat.co.uk**

# HAY HOUSE

*Look within*

Join the conversation about latest products,
events, exclusive offers and more.

 Hay House

 @HayHouseUK

 @hayhouseuk

 healyourlife.com

*We'd love to hear from you!*